HOW TO BECOME A LAWYER?

Cultures juridiques et politiques **Vol. 5**

Les conceptions du pouvoir, du droit et de l'ordre se réfèrent inévitablement à l'ensemble du système de représentations qu'est la culture de chaque société. Toute forme de culture ayant donc nécessairement une dimension politique et juridique, la collection «Cultures juridiques et politiques» publie des travaux, tels que des thèses, synthèses de recherches, ouvrages collectifs et actes de colloques, se proposant de faire connaître les systèmes politiques et juridiques des pays européens, d'évaluer les grandes tendances des processus d'intégration politique et d'harmonisation juridique en cours dans l'Union européenne et d'éclairer les interférences entre le politique, le juridique et les autres aspects «culturels» dans le contexte de ces processus.

IZABELA KRASNICKA &
MAGDALENA PERKOWSKA (ÉDS.)

HOW TO BECOME A LAWYER?

PETER LANG
Bern · Berlin · Bruxelles · Frankfurt am Main · New York · Oxford · Wien

Information bibliographique publiée par
«Die Deutsche Nationalbibliothek»
«Die Deutsche Nationalbibliothek» répertorie cette publication dans la «Deutsche Nationalbibliografie»; les données bibliographiques détaillées sont disponibles sur Internet sous ‹http://dnb.d-nb.de›.

Illustration de la couverture: from iStockphoto.com © by alexsl
Réalisation de couverture: Didier Studer, Peter Lang AG

ISSN 2235-1078 br.
ISBN 978-3-0343-1290-5 br.
ISSN 2235-5952 eBook
ISBN 978-3-0353-0467-1 eBook

Hochfeldstrasse 32, CH-3012 Berne, Suisse
info@peterlang.com, www.peterlang.com

Table of contents

Foreword

The present publication collects the contributions of the colloquium **“How to Become a Lawyer in Europe”,** which took place on June 4, 2010 in Andorra-la Vella – within the framework of the 15th annual meeting of the representatives of the *Network of European Universities in Legal Studies*[1].

In the meetings of this network, which has been initiated and coordinated since 1995 by the director of the *German-French Study Program for Law Students* of the Université Paris Ouest-Nanterre-La Défense, one is attempting to evaluate the activities of the partner universities in terms of student and teacher mobility as well as their scientific cooperation and, of course, to reflect upon how best to further invigorate and broaden all these exchanges in the process of *European Higher Education*, within the so-called “Bologna process”.

The colloquium in Andorra corresponded to the wishes of our Polish colleagues, who during the 14th annual meeting in Sevilla (2009) suggested comparing the national systems for the education of lawyers. Indeed, the opening and deregulation of markets for legal advice within the framework of freedom of service and of movement for lawyers within the common European markets since the mid-1980s has led to fundamental change of the legal profession in all of Europe. The opening of national markets for legal counseling does, of course, not remain without consequences for student attitudes towards their studies and for the educational structures in the individual European countries.

We would like to thank all colleagues who submitted country reports as well as Mr. Joan Miquel Rascagnères, the President of the Andorra Bar Association, and Professor Anna Wyrozumska (Universi-

---

1 For more details, see <http://www.droit-fr-all-paris-ouest.fr/reseau-europeen-de-cooperation-universitaire> (“Network of European Universities in legal studies coordinated by the University of Paris X” 2005) ; <http://www.droit-fr-all-paris-ouest.fr/international> («Réseau européen de coopération universitaire»).

ty of Lodz) for having directed the colloquium. The co-Presidency by Anna Wyrozumska should be seen as an homage to her: one of the most brilliant representatives of the Polish law faculties and thusly a well-seen visiting guest professor at European partner universities, she has earned our deepest thanks and recognition for her vision and engagement in the field of cooperating universities!

Our thanks also go to Professor Stephanie Dijoux (Paris Ouest-Nanterre-La Défense), co-director of the 15th Annual Meeting (Barcelona/Andorra, June 3rd-5th 2010), who provided the contributions from non-European countries (Mauritius) and non-EU countries (Switzerland) for this omnibus volume.

Our special thanks, of course, goes to our Andorran hosts, who have so generously accommodated us during the colloquium. It is a great honor for us to be received by the highest representatives of the state, Justice and the civil society:

The President of the Parliament, Mr. Josep Dalleres Codina,

The Vice-President of the Supreme Court, professor Pierre Subra de Bieusses,

The President of the University of Andorra, professor Daniel Bastida,

The President of the Andorra Bar Association, Mr. Joan Miquel Rascagneres.

And finally, thanks to Mrs. Meritxell Tomàs Baldrich, Secretary General of the Constitutional Court of Andorra, and her colleagues, for the splendid organization of the Colloquium.

Paris, August 2011
Professor Otmar Seul,
Coordinator of the Network of European Universities in legal studies

Preface

The creation of *European Higher Education Area* (EHEA) has been a major advance in promoting convergence in European higher education on our continent, thus making different university systems more comparable and transparent. The EHEA establishes mechanisms that makes the academic recognition of university degrees easier among European countries and promotes the mobility of students from different universities in Europe.

The university degree alone does not guarantee the exercise of certain professions that are regulated in the different states, as in the case of lawyers. For these professions the regulations of diverse European states present very different conditions.

In this respect, the organization of the symposium **"How to Become a Lawyer"** (Andorra la Vella, June 4th) by the *Réseau européen de cooperation universitaire en Sciences juridiques* (*Network of European Universities in Legal Studies*) has been very propitious in highlighting, with academic precision, the diversity of requirements of the various European states.

The University of Andorra and the University of Paris Ouest-Nanterre-La Défense have collaborated in publishing a compilation of the presentations of the colloquium, which show the diversity and complexity of Europe, but at the same time will surely contribute to the understanding of the different requirements needed to become a lawyer.

Professor Daniel Bastida
Rector de la *Universitat d'Andorra*

The Profession of Lawyer in the Principality of Andorra

Joan Miquel RASCAGNERES

The Principality of Andorra, that achieved the legal status of state in 1993 with the approval of its Constitution, places its historical origins in an act named “Els Pareatges”, signed in 1278 by the Bishop of La Seu d’Urgell, a small Spanish city situated in the frontier with Andorra, and the Count of Foix. The rights of the Count of Foix have passed to the President of the French Republic and, today, the Head of state of Andorra is jointly the Bishop of La Seu d’Urgell and the President of the French Republic.

Until the Second World War, Andorra was considered an agricultural society, and accessing the country was very difficult due to the geographical features.

The courts, in their historical form, were created by “Els Pareatges”, in the civil field as well as in the penal one. Nevertheless, until the beginning of the Second World War, no lawyer acted as such in the Principality. Andorrans resorted to the services of those lawyers in La Seu d’Urgell. On the other hand, the University of Andorra was founded approximately twenty years ago and therefore no Andorran could obtain a university degree in the Principality.

It is only after the Second World War that some lawyers from Spain settled in the Principality. Their degree as Lawyer was recognised because they satisfied the conditions required for the exercise of the profession in Spain. Nevertheless, their role was limited.

They could not appear in a penal court. Their duty was covered partly by the “raonadors”, deputies of the Andorran Parliament that assumed the defence of the prosecuted but also the defence of the society.

Before civil courts, the participation of the lawyer was not recognised and they could not sign the causes deposited before the court. These causes were only signed by the parts.

Finally in 1976 the Andorran Parliament that at that time held also the role of the executive power, passed the Decree relative to the liberal professions that established the conditions for the exercise of the profession of lawyer in the Principality of Andorra.

These conditions were inspired by the Spanish legislation in the matter and in consequence required Andorran lawyers to present a degree in Law issued by a Spanish or French university. It was not required any another exam or externship.

At about the same time Andorran lawyers began to appear before criminal courts and gradually, without any text regulating it, they began to sign civil demands.

The Bar Association of the Principality of Andorra was created in 1982 and, shortly after, the Code of Penal Procedure recognised the participation of lawyers during the instructions of the cases and finally, in 1986, an act established that Andorran lawyers could sign civil cases. As from that date until the Constitution, different texts have been published making it compulsory the intervention of the lawyer in penal procedures as well as in civil procedures. Nevertheless, any text modified the conditions set in the Decree of 1976 on liberal professions and, in consequence, for the time being, the exercise of the profession of lawyer is subject to the possession of a master 1 (Bologna Process), equivalent to the old degree of Law Graduate or Master in Law, issued by a state whose diplomas are recognised by the Andorran authorities. To this effect, a committee of technical recognition of the diplomas was created in order to validate the titles issued by foreign universities.

On the other hand, the university of Andorra grants also a degree in Law (máster 1), that allows the registration of the holder in the Bar Association of the Principality of Andorra and therefore the exercise of the profession.

This exercise is subject to the authorization by the Bar Association, which grants such permission upon obtaining, by an Andorran citizen, the degree of Master 1. Foreigners with over 20 years of residence in the Principality can also be granted such authorization.

The Bar Association, conscious of the discrepancies that may exist between these conditions and those valid in other European states, has requested Andorran authorities the modification of the legislation in the matter so that new lawyers are subject to a specialized training during a year. That training would be offered by the university of Andorra, and it would be formed by a Master 2 which would include academic studies and internships.

In fact, young Andorran lawyers have in general, studies made in French or Spanish universities, making it necessary to receive a specialized training in Andorran law. Such training can be offered by the university of Andorra which has already been awarding a diploma in Andorran Law for some years.

There is a project of law under study to such effect, so that in coming years candidates to become lawyers will receive this specialized training during a year, before being able to register in the Bar Association of the Principality of Andorra and before appearing in Andorran courts.

How to become a lawyer in Austria

Ulrike BRANDL

Introduction and legal basis

The Austrian law makes a distinction between the possibility to acquire the qualification to work as a lawyer in Austria and the possibility for a lawyer who acquired the admittance to work as a lawyer in another country to be allowed to work as a lawyer or to provide certain legal services in Austria.

The legal basis regulating the requirements for becoming a lawyer in Austria is the Lawyer's Act (Rechtsanwaltsordnung).[2] The legal basis regulating the possibility for foreign lawyers to be registered in Austria or to provide legal services in Austria is the so called Federal Law on Freedom of Services and the Right of Establishment for European Lawyers and the Provision of Legal Services by Lawyers who are internationally active in Austria.[3] There is a distinction between nationals of the European Economic Area and Switzerland and nationals of the Member States of the Agreement on Trade Related Intellectual Property Rights.

The requirements which have to be fulfilled in order to be allowed to work as a lawyer are enumerated in § 1 Lawyer's Act and specified in Section 1 of the said Act.

---

2 Lawyer's Act (Rechtsanwaltsordnung), FLG 96/1868 as amended.

3 Federal Law on Freedom of Services and the Right of Establishment for European Lawyers and the Provision of Legal Services by Lawyers Acting International in Austria (Bundesgesetz über den freien Dienstleistungsverkehr und die Niederlassung von europäischen Rechtsanwältinnen und Rechtsanwälten sowie die Erbringung von Rechtsdienstleistungen durch international tätige Rechtsanwältinnen und Rechtsanwälte in Österreich), FLG 27/2000 as amended.

The law does not foresee an administrative act which officially confers the accreditation as a lawyer, it is sufficient that the requirements are fulfilled. In case they are fulfilled the person is registered in the official list of lawyers. With the registration the person is allowed to officially work as a lawyer.

The legal basis, which contains the organisation and content of the bar exam is the Lawyer's Examination Act or Bar Exam Act.[4]

Requirements to be fulfilled

The requirements are: 1) necessity to have a certain nationality, 2) finalisation of law studies, 3) five years practice 4) successful completion of the bar exam and 5) participation in certain training seminars. The law also contains an obligation to effect a liability insurance.

Necessity to have a certain nationality

The person who intends to be registered as a lawyer in Austria has to possess Austrian nationality or the nationality of a Member State of the European Economic Area or Switzerland.

Finalisation of law studies

Finalisation of law studies means that the person has obtained a masters degree in law in Austria, which is acquired after the successful completion of diploma studies (Diplomstudium) with a minimum duration of four years and the workload of 240 ECTS credits. It is required that certain fields of law are contained in the curriculum. The candidate has to show that he or she finished with positive exams.

4 Lawyer's Examination Act or Bar Exam Act (Rechtsanwaltsprüfungsgesetz), FLG 556/1985 as amended.

Obligatory legal subjects are Austrian civil law and civil procedures law, Austrian criminal law and criminal procedures law, Austrian administrative law and administrative procedures law, constitutional law including human rights protection, public international law, European law, employment and social law, tax law, business law and other fields of law and economy. Within the legal studies it is required that the person has to write a diploma work or a similar scientific essay showing the ability to scientific legal research and work.

It is not possible to become a lawyer with a bachelor degree. So far the curricula at Austrian universities do not provide for bachelor degrees in law. There is only the possibility to obtain master degrees. It is however possible to obtain a bachelor degree in studies such as law and economy or similar. These bachelor degrees require a minimum duration of studies of six semesters. Usually there is the possibility to continue these studies and obtain a master degree. These degrees neither bachelor nor master are however sufficient in order to allow the person to become a lawyer. It is not possible to become a lawyer with a degree "Master on law and economy" or with a similar degree. § 3 Lawyer's Act requires law studies.

Up to now the "Bologna rules" have not been implemented as far as law studies are concerned. There are contacts between the Universities and the bar associations preparing the implementation. It is most likely that a master degree will be required, a bachelor degree will not be sufficient in order to be registered as a lawyer.

It is necessary that the law studies have been conducted in Austria or in another Member State of the European Union or in Switzerland, provided that the studies are equivalent. The studies have to comprise at least 240 ECTS credits. The question if studies are equivalent has to be decided on the basis of the provisions of the so called Law on Crediting of Apprenticeship and Vocational Assessment or Training and Professional Examination Credit Law (Ausbildungs- und Berufsprüfungsanrechnungsgesetz).[5] Austrian practice follows the

5 Law on Crediting of Apprenticeship and Vocational Assessment or Training and Professional Examination Credit Law (Ausbildungs- und Berufsprüfungsanrechnungsgesetz).

Morgenbesser Judgement of the Court of Justice of the European Union.[6] According to the judgement it is required that the competent authority examines whether, and to what extent, "the knowledge certified by the diploma granted in another Member State and the qualifications or professional experience obtained there, together with the experience obtained in the Member State in which the candidate seeks enrolment, must be regarded as satisfying, even partially, the conditions required for access to the activity concerned".[7] If the requirements are only partly fulfilled the person has to obtain the additional qualifications in Austria. In case it is not sufficiently clear that the studies are equivalent a committee established with the bar association together with the assistance of the chairman of the Commission responsible for organizing and taking bar exams may ask for an advisory opinion of a University professor. Professors also serve as examiners according to the so called Bar Exam Act.

Five years practice

The Lawyer's Act requires five years practice. The practice has to comprise a minimum duration of nine months at Courts and three years working with a lawyer resp. in the law firm of a registered lawyer. Practice at courts is available for everybody who finished law studies in Austria or equivalent studies in a Member State of the European Economic Area or in Switzerland. Practice has to be on a full time basis. If a person only works part time this time may be recognised if it is at least half time of regular work. Only the factual work time is counted. If a person only works part time the period required prolongs. Practice requirements have to be fulfilled after the person completed law studies. The remaining time counted from five years in total minus three years and nine months may be fulfilled also with working at Courts or with a lawyer. The candidate may also complete

6 ECJ, Judgment of 13 November 2003, C-313/01, Morgenbesser v. Consiglio dell'Ordine degli avvocati di Genova.

7 Supra, para. 67.

practice with another judicial work, e.g. with public authorities, at Universities or also with studies at a University, where a further academic degree in law is acquired (a maximum period of six months is counted).

The successful completion of the bar exam

The candidate has to undergo a written and oral exam called bar exam. § 4 Lawyer's Act requires that the candidate successfully passes the bar exam. The organisation, conditions and the content of the exam are regulated by a specific law called Lawyer's Examination Act or Bar Exam Act (Rechtsanwaltsprüfungsgesetz).[8] It is possible to take the bar exam after three years practice (9 months at courts, 2 years with a registered lawyer), the registration as a lawyer however is only possible after five years. The bar exam comprises three written exams, each eight hours. The subjects are criminal law, civil law, constitutional and administrative law. If the candidate successfully passed these exams there is a subsequent oral exam of 4 hours. The examination is taken by a panel of two lawyers and two judges.
After five years and after the final successful bar exam the person may ask for registration as a lawyer (official list, bar association).

Participation in certain training seminars

The future lawyer has to participate in specific courses which are held for the purpose to educate lawyers and according to the guidelines to train lawyers. The maximum duration is 42 half day seminars.

8 See fn. 3.

Requirements for lawyers, who acquired the accreditation to work as a lawyer in another country, to be registered as a lawyer in Austria or to be allowed to work as a lawyer in Austria

There is a distinction between nationals of Member States of the European Economic Area and Switzerland who acquired the qualification and admittance to work as a lawyer in their country of nationality and between nationals of a Member State of the Agreement on Trade related Intellectual Property Rights, who acquired this qualification in their home country. The first category is called European Lawyers, the second one International Lawyers or Lawyers who are internationally active. A European lawyer (who has the official qualification as a lawyer in his or her home country or another country) may be allowed to work as a lawyer in Austria. It is possible either if the person has already worked as a lawyer in Austria for three years (with a registered lawyer) or if the person passes an exam showing that the person is qualified to work as a lawyer (*Eignungstest*). Even before the person is officially recognised as a lawyer including registry with the bar association (list of European Lawyers) persons who qualify as a lawyer in another state are allowed to work as a lawyer in Austria. They however have to use the official title granted in their country. If they intend to represent a client in proceedings where a lawyer is obligatory they need an Austrian lawyer as a partner (*Einvernehmensanwalt*). The law provides for a registration in a list of European lawyers.

International lawyers are allowed to provide certain legal services if they fulfil the conditions. The possibilities to provide legal services are very limited. They are enumerated in Art. 40 Federal Law on Freedom of Services and the Right of Establishment for European Lawyers and the Provision of Legal Services by Lawyers Acting International in Austria.[9] These lawyers are allowed to legal counseling concerning the legal situation in their country of origin and concerning International Law (except Law of the European Union). The lawyers have to inform the bar association about their activities. They have to

---

9 See fn. 2.

use the official title granted in their country and have to show their membership in a bar association.

How to become a lawyer in the Czech Republic

Martin KOPA, Maxim TOMOSZEK

Legal Education in the Czech Republic

The basic requirement for all traditional legal professions in the Czech Republic is obtaining of a Master degree in Law. The Master study program takes five years.[10] In order to be accepted to Master study program, the students must successfully pass the maturity exam, which typically comes after 9 years of elementary school and 4 years of secondary school. Recently, a uniform maturity exam was introduced for all secondary schools, but most universities still prefer another type of admission exam. The admission tests for Master study program in Law typically consist of two parts – one is focused on general social sciences background and the other tests general qualification for university study.

The content and structure of Master study programs was until recently relatively unified on all four public Law Faculties (Brno, Olomouc, Pilsen, Prague). The first year was dedicated to mostly non-law subjects and basic law subjects (history, psychology, sociology, philosophy, theory of law and roman law), the second and third year were dedicated to core subjects of public and private law (civil law, civil procedure, family law, criminal law, criminal procedure, constitutional law, administrative law, administrative procedure), and the fourth and fifth year usually offered public and private international law, more specialized subjects (labor law, social security law, tax law) and elective courses.

10 For more information of university education in the Czech Republic, see Act No. 111/1998 Coll., on universities, as amended.

The studies were (and still are) concluded by writing and defending a master thesis and on most faculties also by state exams in the main legal subjects.

This model of law studies did not significantly change in last 100 years and is often subject of debate among legal professionals and academics today. The most problematic features of law studies are its focus on non-law subjects in the first year and emphasis on theoretical knowledge. The Law Faculty of the Palacký University in Olomouc has reformed its Master study program in Law in 2009, starting with the first year of the new program in 2010, and a similar, but less intensive reform was carried out by the Law Faculty of the Masaryk University in Brno in 2010. The reformed program in Olomouc was designed in cooperation with experts from different legal professions, future employers and students, which mainly resulted in more focus on legal subjects, practical application of knowledge and skills development. The structure of compulsory subjects in the reformed program is the following:

First Year			
Constitutional History	(36 hrs.)	Introduction to Public Law	(24 hrs.)
Constitutional Law	(48 hrs.)	Roman Law	(96 hrs.)
Economy	(36 hrs.)	Study Skills	(36 hrs.)
Foreign Language	(96 hrs.)	Theory of Law	(60 hrs.)
Human Rights	(36 hrs.)		
Introduction to Private Law	(96 hrs.)		
Second year			
Administrative Law	(48 hrs.)	European Law	(60 hrs.)
Civil Law	(96 hrs.)	Foreign Language	(48 hrs.)
Civil Procedure	(48 hrs.)	Human Rights	(48 hrs.)
Corporate Law	(72 hrs.)		
Criminal Law	(96 hrs.)		
Third year			
Administrative Law	(96 hrs.)	Law of Contract	(96 hrs.)
Civil Procedure	(72 hrs.)	Legal Methodology	(36 hrs.)
Criminal Law	(48 hrs.)	Legal Skills Course	(24 hrs.)
International Public Law	(48 hrs.)	Stocks and Bonds	(12 hrs.)
Labour Law	(60 hrs.)		
Fourth year			
Administrative Law	(48 hrs.)	International Private Law	(36 hrs.)
Applied Criminal Law	(24 hrs.)	Law of Succession	(24 hrs.)
Competition Law	(18 hrs.)	Legal Philosophy	(36 hrs.)
Environmental Law	(72 hrs.)	Legal Research and Writing	(12 hrs.)
Family Law	(48 hrs.)	Social Security Law	(36 hrs.)
Financial Law	(96 hrs.)		
Fifth Year			
Administrative Justice	(48 hrs.)	Thesis Seminar	(12 hrs.)
Law of Intellectual Property	(24 hrs.)		

There are also more than 100 elective courses in the Master program, which allow the students to focus in more detail on specific areas of law with regard to their future practice orientation. Some of the courses are aligned into modules, which allow student to acquire specialization in the diploma supplement.

The structure of legal studies, even with recently introduced changes, means that the Czech Law Faculties did not fully implement the Bologna Process. The three year Bachelor study programs in Law do exist, but the follow-up two year Master programs do not. This means that the Bachelor degree is usually designed as a specialized study for officers of public administration or paralegals. It could be also useful in combination with two years Master programs outside law, such as economy, management, politics or journalism.

However, for the five main legal professions in the Czech Republic (judge, state prosecutor, attorney, notary and executor), it is required to finish the five year Master program in Law. All these professions also have a special training system, which includes apprenticeship or practice and exams. All these five main professions are to certain degree compatible, because fulfillment of practice or examination in one of these professions also counts as fulfillment of practice or examination in other professions. However, all professions with exception of attorneys have only a limited number of places, determined by state, and are usually subject to selection procedure.

There are also other legal professions, like lawyer of a business corporation, tax advisor, lawyer in state administration, lawyer in NGO etc., which do not require any special training or exam and may require only Bachelor degree in Law.

Becoming a Judge in the Czech Republic

Conditions for becoming a judge in the Czech Republic are currently regulated by Act No. 6/2002 Coll., on Courts, Judges, Lay Judges and the State Administration of Courts and on the amendments to some other Acts, as amended (so-called Courts and Judges Act, hereinafter "CJA"). It sets forth a number of conditions that every law school graduate has to fulfill in order to become a judge in civil law, criminal law or administrative law branch of the Czech judiciary.

Both professional judges and lay judges must be Czech citizens, they must have full legal capacity, no criminal record (i.e., without conviction of a premeditated criminal act) and they must have gained such experience and moral characteristics which secure proper performance of the position of a (lay) judge. Furthermore, they must be of at least thirty years of age, they must consent to the appointment to the position of (lay) judge and comply with other conditions and moral requirements given by the law.

Apart from the lay judges who decide only in cases specified by the law, e.g. in labor law ones, professional judges have to satisfy two more requirements: obtaining a legal education (Master – Mgr.) at one of the Czech universities and then every candidate has to pass the judicial exam. Before a candidate is admitted to the judicial exam, he/she has to accomplish three years of practice as a judicial trainee after being successful in a selection procedure. However, Czech judicial system is open and it allows trainees, assistants of judges and law clerks from other branches of the legal profession to attend judicial exam in case they have achieved three years of practice. Judicial exams test theoretical and practical knowledge of the trainee and they also include psychological-diagnostic test, all of which demand long and thorough preparation.

Judicial trainees usually co-operate with professional judges, they provide them with legal research and participate on minor decision-making, e.g. in obvious procedural issues. Trainees do not work with only one judge during whole traineeship. They actually circulate among various departments of the court where their traineeship takes place. As mentioned above, the traineeship is three years long and its current state is highly criticized for non-conceptuality because after law school graduation which is usually achieved at 24 or 25 years of age and undergoing the three years long traineeship finished with a judicial exam there is a vacuum period of up to three years in which the candidate is fully competent but has to wait until the thirtieth birthday in order to be eligible for judge appointment.

Notwithstanding that, if the judicial candidate fulfills all the requirements given by the law, the President of respective Regional Court submits a list of prospective candidates to the Ministry of Justice. Subsequently, Minister of Justice proposes their appointment to the President of the Czech Republic who under Czech Constitution finally appoints the candidates to the position of judges for life. As already stated above, Czech judicial system is open and therefore even attorneys, notaries and other legal professionals may be appointed as judges if they have passed respective professional exam and fulfill other legal requirements for the position of a judge. It is permitted, because just like the practice, even professional exams are acknowledged and regarded as equal to the judicial exam. Lay judges are elected for a four years long period by municipal and regional councils. State Administration of the courts is carried out by the Ministry of Justice.

After being appointed to a particular court, judge is assigned to a particular agenda under the work schedule and his/her judicial career is thus commenced. However, the current system of requirements for the position of a judge has been regarded as inappropriate by the experts, therefore there might be significant changes coming in the next couple of years.

In case a professional lawyer desires to become a judge of the Constitutional Court, he/she must fulfill conditions set in the Czech Constitution and the Act No. 182/1993 Coll., on the Constitutional Court, as amended (hereinafter "ACC"). The required age limit is 40 years of age and besides having no criminal record and being legally educated, candidates for the position of a constitutional judge must have 10 years long legal practice. Constitutional judges are appointed by the President of the Czech Republic with approval of the Senate.

Becoming a State Prosecutor in the Czech Republic

Regulation of how to become a state prosecutor in the Czech Republic is set in Act No. 283/1993 Coll., on State Prosecution, as amended (hereinafter "ASP"). The purpose of State Prosecution which is constitutionally classified as part of the Executive is to represent the state in protection of public interest in cases provided by the law. These cases in majority comprise of representing state in criminal proceedings. Nevertheless, State Prosecution also operates in civil proceedings, e.g. in paternity cases.

Conditions for becoming a state prosecutor are very similar to the conditions for becoming a judge with one big exception – the age limit is only 25 years. Therefore future state prosecutors do not have to face such discrepancies as judicial candidates. But apart from this particular requirement, they have to fulfill pretty much the same conditions as judges. Likewise, they must have full legal capacity, no criminal record and they must have gained such experience and moral characteristics which secure proper performance of the position of a state prosecutor. Obviously, they must have obtained a legal education (Master – Mgr.) at one of the Czech universities and after three years long traineeship, every candidate has to pass the final exam. Successful passing of a different legal professional exam is also equally acknowledged and before appointment, it must be approved by the Minister of Justice.

After candidates pass the final exam, the Supreme State Prosecutor proposes a list of candidates to the Minister of Justice who is in charge of the appointment under ASP. Following the appointment, state prosecutors are assigned to a specific state prosecutor's office, where they engage in activities reserved for the state prosecutors by respective laws. The whole system of Public Prosecution is further supervised by Ministry of Justice which has a competency to secure the functioning of Public Prosecution and its organizational, personal and economical aspects.

Becoming an Attorney in the Czech Republic

As far as the regulation of working as an attorney in the Czech Republic is concerned, it is provided by the Act no. 85/1996 Coll., on Advocacy, as amended (hereinafter "AA"). Attorneys are also bound by internal regulations of the Czech Bar Association which is responsible for self-administration of this profession. Generally speaking, we might observe that it is the mostly chosen profession by fresh graduates. Many students even work as paralegals and assistants in law firms during their university studies.

First stage to be completed before a lawyer becomes an attorney with full authority to represent clients before all courts and to provide unlimited advocacy services is the apprenticeship. During this stage, the articled clerk registered at the Bar Association works under supervision of an attorney who is full member of the Bar and gradually prepares himself/herself for the Bar exam. The apprenticeship period must be at least three years long and at the end of it, the articled clerk ought to be familiar with all practical and theoretical aspects of this profession. However, there are certain areas of practice where articled clerks are not allowed to participate, e.g. before the Constitutional Court. Nonetheless, the apprenticeship is concluded by a Bar Exam which belongs to the group of the most challenging and really hard exams to pass.

If the Bar Exam is successfully passed, attorneys may decide whether they are going to practice individually or as employees of a law firm. It must be noted that top attorneys have very high salaries which is usually one of the primary reasons of choosing this profession after graduating from law school. On the other hand, it is very stressful job with high responsibility and personal requirements. Lately, attorneys have been dealing with intense competition because this profession continually gets more and more crowded, as well (currently, there are approximately 9.500 attorneys and 3.300 lawyers in apprenticeship in the Czech Republic). Approximately half of the attorneys are based in Prague.

Czech Bar Association secures the standards of providing advocacy services by organizing compulsory education for its (registered) members and also by issuing internal regulations. Association has six bodies including disciplinary committee which decides on alleged misconducts of attorneys, e.g. breaches of the ethical code. To end with a little curiosity, it has been enacted not too long ago that since June 2011, attorneys will face long discussed novelty – obligatory wearing of a gown in court in certain cases. There is also serious discussion about prolonging the apprenticeship period to total of 5 years.

Becoming a Notary in the Czech Republic

Notaries are legal professionals, who were entrusted by the state with providing certain legal services, such as drawing up official protocols verifying certain facts, writing wills and other legal documents, authenticating legal documents and depositing legal documents or money. Notaries can also provide legal advice and provide representation at court in certain types of proceedings. They can also manage property and provide legal service connected to insolvency. Each notary has his office, where he may employ notary candidates, notary apprentices and other employees.

According to the Act No. 358/1992 Coll., on Notaries and their operation, as amended, in order to become a notary, one has to be the citizen of the Czech Republic, possess full legal capacity, obtain Master degree in Law, have no criminal record, have fulfilled a five-year notary practice and successfully passed the notary exam. The five-year notary practice is usually fulfilled in the form of apprenticeship in a notary office, but can be also fulfilled by practice in other profession.

However, the connection of this profession with the state also means, that there is only a limited number of offices in each region. Totally, there are approximately 500 notary offices in the Czech Republic, one for approximately 20,000 citizens. Notaries are appointed by Minister of Justice based on proposal of the professional association of notaries, which selects the candidates based on public selection procedure. So after fulfillment of all the above-mentioned criteria, one does not automatically become a notary, but rather a notary candidate. In practice it means that the candidates have to wait until an existing notary place becomes vacant (e.g. the former notary dies, resigns or retires) and then sign up for the selection procedure. In the meantime, they usually work in a notary office of other notary.

Becoming an Executor in the Czech Republic

The profession of executor is a relatively new profession, as it was brought into life in year 2001 by Act No. 120/2001 Coll., on executors and executions, as amended. The main aim of executors is to carry out executions, i.e. forced realization of debts and other execution warrants. They can also provide legal advice, drawing up documents, depositing legal documents or money and serving court documents. Each executor has his office, where he may employ executor candidates, executor apprentices, dispensers and other employees.

In order to become an executor, one has to be the citizen of the Czech Republic, possess full legal capacity, obtain Master degree in Law, have no criminal record, have fulfilled a three-year executors' practice and successfully passed the executors' exam. The three-year executors' practice is usually fulfilled in the form of apprenticeship in an executor's office, but can be also fulfilled by practice in other profession.

Again, there is only a limited number of executors' offices. The number of executors was recently raised to approximately 200, one for approximately 50,000 citizens. Executors are appointed by Minister of Justice based on public selection procedure carried out by the Ministry of Justice. So after fulfillment of all the above-mentioned criteria, one does not automatically become an executor, but rather an executor candidate. In practice it means that the candidates have to wait until an existing executor's place becomes vacant (e.g. the former executor dies, resigns or retires) and then sign up for the selection procedure. In the meantime, they usually work in an executor's office.

Other legal professions

Apart from all the legal professions already mentioned and regulated by special laws, there are several other professions which might be described as legal though they do not require legal education formally but rather materially. Occupations that may be classed here subsume lawyers who work in Legislature or Executive, diplomats, arbitrators, mediators etc.

Committees of all kinds within the framework of Legislature and Executive allow lawyers to participate in the process of law-making and securing proper functioning of the Public Administration. Every ministry has a legal department which deals with legal aspects of their operation and they also prepare proposals for secondary legislation. These lawyers are involved in so-called amendment procedure which precedes finalizations of bills. Both chambers of the Czech Parliament have legislative departments, as well. For example, they submit paragraphed version of draft codes for enactment and opinions on them. All these lawyers are employees of the state and thus they contribute to the Public Service.

Lawyers who are specialized in public international law might also serve as diplomats and members of diplomatic missions. However, inter-governmental relations require mainly specific personal abilities and negotiation skills where being an international public law expert is not a necessity.

Many legal professionals may act as arbitrators in arbitral proceedings because Act no. 216/1994 Coll., on arbitration and the enforcement of arbitration awards, as amended, is not strict in conditions required for the position of an arbitrator. Every adult Czech citizen who has full legal capacity may serve as an arbitrator as well as every foreigner who has full legal capacity under laws of his/her country and therefore many lawyers accept arbitrator nominations by the parties to the dispute seeking its resolution in arbitration. Moreover, all the means of alternative dispute resolution, such as mediation, mini-trial, medaloa etc., offer ideal opportunity for lawyers to practice law alongside their primary profession.

List of these professions is certainly not definite because undoubtedly, there a lot more possibilities and options for graduate lawyers. They may work as commercial lawyers, tax advisors, in-house counsels and so on. To sum up briefly, we might conclude that law school graduation opens quite a wide spectrum of job opportunities which gives lawyers a significant advantage in comparison to other university graduates.

Becoming a lawyer in England and Wales

Anthony DURSI

The United Kingdom comprises three distinct legal jurisdictions: England & Wales, Scotland and Northern Ireland. This article will outline the steps required in order to become a lawyer in England and Wales.

England and Wales is a common law jurisdiction with a split legal profession: the overarching term "lawyer" encompasses solicitors, barristers and legal executives. The solicitor side of the profession is much larger, with nearly 118,000 practising solicitors in 2010,[11] which compares to just over 15,000 practising barristers.[12] Solicitors are generally the first point of contact for clients, and are generally office-based whereas barristers specialise in courtroom advocacy and giving expert legal opinions.

Qualifying as either a solicitor or barrister can be divided into three main stages: academic, vocational and professional. The academic stage is the same for both sides of the profession, but it is important to consider these different routes at an early stage in order to undertake relevant work experience. Qualification as a legal executive follows a different path, with no university degree necessary.

---

11 The Law Society Annual Report 2010, <http://www.lawsociety.org.uk/secure/file/191440/e:/teamsite-deloyed/documents/templatedata/Publications/Research%20Publications/Documents/annualstatreport2010.pdf>.

12 The Bar Council Bar Barometer, March 2011, <http://www.barcouncil.org.uk/assets/documents/Bar%20Barometer,%20March%202011.pdf>.

Solicitor

Academic stage

Many students undertake a qualifying law degree at undergraduate level most often in the form of a LLB. Qualifying law degrees are widely available at UK institutions (a full list of providers can be found on the Solicitor Regulation Authority's website[13]) and they are usually three years in duration. Alternatively, students can do an undergraduate degree in any subject other than law, and then complete the year long conversion course – the Graduate Diploma in Law (GDL) or Common Professional Examination (CPE).

Vocational stage

Upon graduation, those wishing to qualify as a solicitor must undertake a legal skills course, the Legal Practice Course (LPC). This is usually completed over one year full time but can also be done part time over two years, allowing prospective solicitors to combine it with work. Fees for the LPC range from approximately £9,000 to £13,000, but these fees are covered by the law firms for those who have managed to secure a training contract prior to starting the LPC.

Professional stage

Known as a training contract, this is a two-year period of training with a law firm, allowing for further skills development in a working environment. This is usually divided into four six-month blocks in different departments (known as "seats"), although in smaller firms this may not be so structured. The minimum salary for 2011-12 is £16,650

---

13 <http://www.sra.org.uk/students/courses/Qualifying-law-degree-providers.page>.

(£18,590 in Central London), although large commercial firms in London can pay considerably more. During the training contract, trainees must also complete a Professional Skills Course, which comprises a series of modules and exams and takes 12 days if completed full-time. Many law firms recruit their trainee solicitors two years in advance, so law students need to be researching and making applications to these firms before the end of their second year at university (and non-law students need to do the same before the end of their final year).

Admission to the Roll

Once the degree, Legal Practice Course, Professional Skills Course and training contact have all been completed, an application can be made to the roll of solicitors in England and Wales, which entitles the individual to practise as a solicitor.

Barrister

Academic stage

As with aspiring solicitors, those wishing to qualify as barristers must also complete either a qualifying law degree or a conversion course.

Vocational stage

Upon completion of the above, students must take an additional one year full-time (or two year part-time) course – the Bar Professional Training Course (BPTC). This is taught at 11 providers across the UK, and costs between £11,000 and £16,500. Prior to joining, students must join one of the Inns of Court – Inner Temple, Middle Temple,

Gray's Inn or Lincoln's Inn, all of which have scholarships available to help towards the cost of the BPTC. During the BPTC, students must complete 12 qualifying sessions at their chosen Inn of Court, which can range from topical legal residential weekends to lecture nights.

Professional stage

Aspiring barristers have five years from their Call to the Bar date (the ceremony at their Inn of Court which marks the completion of the BPTC) to obtain pupillage. This is a one-year period of practical training in Chambers or at an authorised Pupillage Training Organisation at the Employed Bar, which could range from a solicitors firm to the Crown Prosecution Service or Government Legal Service. Pupillage is divided into two parts: the non-practising six months (also known as the first six) and the practising six months (also known as the second six). Pupils must complete advocacy, ethics and practice management training during pupillage in order to obtain their full qualification certificate. Pupils are paid a minimum of £12,000 for the year, but some top commercial sets pay up to £65,000. Earnings for both pupils and practicing barristers vary considerably by practice area, with commercial and civil practitioners normally able to earn substantially more than their criminal and family counterparts.

Tenancy

Following pupillage, barristers who want to work in self-employed practice seek tenancy at a set of chambers, usually in the set in which they completed pupillage. Getting "tenancy" means being accepted as a permanent member of that set of chambers, usually by means of a vote by other members of chambers. Unsuccessful pupils often go on to complete a "third six" pupillage at another set or, less commonly, obtain tenancy elsewhere.

Barristers who complete their pupillage in employed practice will typically seek permanent employment with the organization that trained them, although they may choose to apply to another organization or to chambers. Equally, barristers who completed pupillage in chambers may wish to move into employed practice.

Whilst self-employed practitioners make up 80% of the Bar, some prefer to work as an employed barrister, which pays a salary and offers a substantially different working practice. Recent changes brought about by the Legal Services Act may mean that in the future barristers will be able to work as both employed and self-employed practitioners.

Legal Executive

Academic stage

The Institute of Legal Executives (ILEX) is the professional body that governs the education and training of legal executives. With no prior law qualifications, the academic part of the ILEX training program is made up of two stages of training: the ILEX Level 3 Professional Diploma in Law and Practice and the ILEX Level 6 Professional Higher Diploma in Law and Practice. The two stages are both typically studied part-time over two years, and together cost approximately £6,200. ILEX also now offers a Graduate Fast Track Diploma for those with a qualifying law degree, which involves the study of two ILEX Level 6 Practice Units and costs £1910. With part-time study, this route to qualification allows trainees to work in a legal setting, potentially contributing to their qualifying employment requirements.

Professional stage

In order to become a recognized "legal executive", a total of five years' qualifying employment must be completed. At least two years must be completed after the academic stage, and must be consecutive. Qualifying employment includes carrying out work of a legal nature under the supervision of a solicitor, senior legal executive, barrister or licensed conveyancer. Employment can be in legal practice, in the legal department of a private company or in local/national government.

Following successful completion of qualifying employment, which is undertaken under the supervision of a solicitor, legal executives can apply to the roll of solicitors in England and Wales, allowing them to practise as a solicitor.

How to become a lawyer in France

Stephanie DIJOUX

The lawyer's profession is a noble one. His contribution to the administration of justice is often underestimated. Yet, he is an indispensable element in the assurance that the justice is not only done but seen to be done. The lawyer is a part of the judiciary and as such is engaged in the same concern that is the search for truth. So he should not only represent the interest of his client but also not forget his duty which he owes to the justice and his obligation not to hide the truth[14]. So, professional ethic is very important for lawyers in France.

The role of a lawyer in France is varied and wide area. The former distinction between a lawyer (*avocet*) and a barrister (*avoué*) doesn't exist anymore.

Lawyers practicing today in France have to be specialist in drafting and procedures. They can give legal advice and have the right of audience before all courts (except the Supreme Court, *Conseil d'Etat* and the Constitutional Court, where only specially admitted lawyers can appear). The lawyer is bound by a contract with his client.

The role of the lawyer as a defense counsel is to safeguard and promote the interests of the accused party within the limits permitted by the ethics of his profession. He will do the best to ensure that his client has a fair trial and that the rules of procedure and evidence are not infringed to the detriment of the client. He should defend the client to the best of his ability, but he has a duty towards the Court.

In the light of globalization we need also high level lawyers able to cope with the international demands. This implies specialized business and financial lawyers. More and more lawyers will have to consider the necessity of specialization.

---

14 Justice Campton, Call of duty, 2008.

The system of professional legal training must face these requirements.

In France, there are mainly three possibilities to become a lawyer:

I. the admission by a postgraduate legal qualification;
II. the admission of other legal professions with a requirement of more or less years of professional experiences in the legal field;
III. the admission by the free movement of lawyers in.

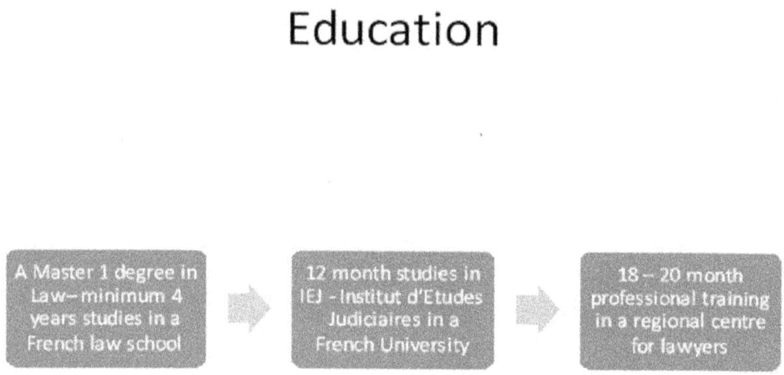

Figure 1: Education

The admission by a postgraduate legal qualification

Lawyers are requested to have a law degree before taking the vocational examinations. In France they need at least a Master 1 degree obtained after 4 years studies in a french law school.

After completion of the Master 1 degree, the futur lawyers need to be first succesfull in the exmination to enter into the professional scool. The admission is conditioned in the success of an entrance examination organized by a university or in the ownership of a doctorate degree in law. The examinations are organized by the Institutes of

Judicial Studies (IEJ– *Institut d'Etudes Judiciaires*) present within every University. Students have to complete 12 month studies in this institute to prepare the entrance examination of the professional scool.

Examination to enter into professional schools

The examination is divides in a admissibility and a admission part. The admissibility part consists in a writing of a summary memorandum and a written examination to evaluate the level of understanding and knowledge of legal issues of the applicant.

The admission part consist in a oral examination of civil and human rights and in additional oral tests (private law, public law) and an oral examination in foreign language.

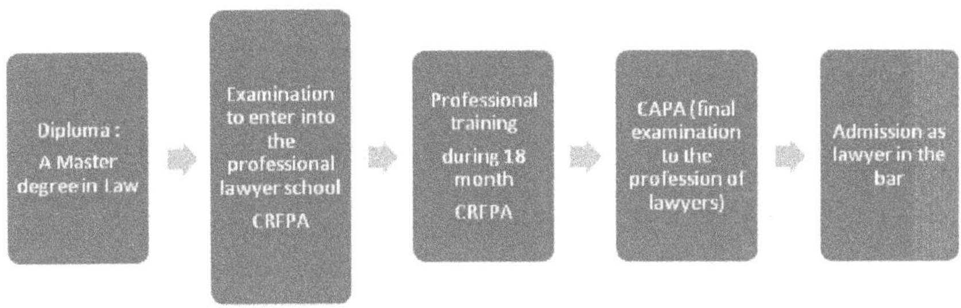

Figure 2: Education

Professional training

The professional scool in France, a regional center of vocational training of lawyers (CRFPA) is a school loaded with the vocational training of lawyers.

The regional centres of vocational training of lawyers prepare in 18 – 20 months for the examination for the postgraduate legal qualification (CAPA).

We count in metropolitan France and in french overseas departements fifteen schools of lawyers, distributed according to the competences of Court of Appeal.

After Admission in the regional centre of vocational training (CRFPA), the professional training is completed at less during 18 month (3 periods of 6 months each).

It consists in 6 month fundamental courses at the bar school and other 6 month courses in the bar school or apprenticeship in a jurisdiction and at least a 6 month apprenticeship in a law firm.

After this period of apprenticeship the future lawyer needs to obtain the examination for the postgraduate legal qualification (CAPA).

He then takes the oath in front of the Court of Appeal and joins the bar.

Admission of other legal professions

There are two different ways of admission of other legal professions in respect of the professional experience of the applicant.

One way concerns the extensive exemption: the exemption from the request of a diploma, the professional training and the vocational examination. This is only applicable for judges, law professors and members of the highest law courts in France.[15]

15 Article 97 du décret du 27 November 1991: Are liberated from the request of a diploma (master degree in law), the professional training and the final examination for admission to the profession of lawyers:

I. Members of "Conseil d'Etat" and judges of administrative courts
II. Magistrates of financial courts (Court of auditors «Cour des comptes et chambres régional des comptes»)
III. Judges of ordinary courts
IV. Law professors

The second way concerns an exemption for members of other legal professions with enough professional experience[16]. This exemption concerns the request of the professional training and the vocational examination. The request of the diploma is maintained.

Free movement of lawyers in Europe

Each Country has its own legal system. Europe has adopted the civil code derived mainly from the Roman law. English law has a Saxon origin with a sprinkling of French law. The different origins and traditions of the legal systems in Europe need specialized lawyers for each country of the European community.

But every lawyer, member of a country of the European Union, is entitled to practice law in France only if he fulfils the requirements pertaining to professional degree established by the law in his country and he works as a legal professional under the original title in the country where the person obtained the legal qualification (Rechtsanwalt)[17].

---

16 Article 98 du décret du 27 November 199: Are liberated from the request of the professional training (CRFPA) and the final examination for admission to the profession of lawyers:

I. Notaries, bailiffs, Counsel in industrial property, with at least 5 years professional practice;
II. Lecturers (Maitre de conférence), assistant lecturers - holder of a PhD with at less 5 years of teaching experience in a department of law;
III. Corporate in-house counsel with at less 8 years professional practice in a law department;
IV. Government officials with at least 8 years professional practice in law in a public service or an international organisation.

17 Article 99 du décret du 27 November 1991 (directive 89/48/CEE): EU-lawyers shall be entitled to practice law in France only if they fulfil the requirements pertaining to professional degree established by the law in their country; Working

Ability test for european lawyers

Every Lawyer, who wants to work in France as a French lawyer under the title "*avocat à la cour*" needs to complete the ability test for European lawyers held by the local bar association.

The ability test consists of at most for law fields: Private law, criminal law, public law, deontology, which are divided in 3 oral and one written examinations. Exemptions could be given in respect of subjects already covered in the obtaining of foreign degrees. Each case has to be considered on its own merits by a specific committee in the light of the performance of the applicant. Every applicant needs to complete the deontology examination without exemption.
No person can try more than 3 times the ability test.

---

as a legal professional under the original titre in the country where the person obtained the legal qualification *("Rechtsanwalt")*.

How to become a lawyer in Germany

Claudia SCHLÜTER

Legal education in Germany has always been subject to strong discussions[18] especially with regard to the Bologna process.[19] Traditional legal education in Germany is provided by Universities whereas the final examination is offered by the ministry of justice, that is to say, by the state. Thus regarding the traditional education there has been no University degree for law students. This system has slightly changed since 2003 when a compulsory University examination was introduced[20]. But like a single swallow does not make a summer this reform was only a very little step towards the Bologna process. Many concepts have been discussed in order to implement the Bologna system into legal education – and, in some respect, it worked out as one can see below.

Law studies at University

The traditional legal education starts with at least eight semesters of law studies at University.[21] Students are obliged to take exams in the main fields of law: civil law, criminal law, constitutional law, administrative law and procedural law. All subjects are taught with reference

18 Verhandlungen des 25. Deutschen Juristentages 1900/1901, pp. 89–117, 223–234.

19 Pfeiffer, NJW 2005, 2281–2283; Jeep, NJW 2005, pp. 2283–2286; BVerfGE, NVwZ-RR 2008, S. 33f.

20 Gesetz zur Reform der Juristenausbildung vom 11.07.2002, BGBl. I p. 2592.

21 § 5 a I Deutsches Richtergesetz <http://www.gesetze-im-internet.de/bundesrecht/drig/gesamt.pdf>, 04.12.2012.

to European law. In addition to that, students take courses in law and language, in methodology of law, in legal history and in philosophy of law. Moreover they are obliged to take courses in key qualifications (*Schlüsselqualifikationen*).

These are, for example, mediation, rhetoric or negotiation. The aim is on the one hand to ensure that students will be able to transfer their knowledge into practice. On the other hand it is part of the implementation of the lifelong learning programme introduced by Decision 1720/2006/EC of the European Parliament and of the Council[22] in 2006. In order to gain practical experience students have to take part in an internship of at least three months. All these contents mentioned above are laid down by federal law – *Deutsches Richtergesetz* (DRiG).

Following this framework the 16 German states (*Länder*) laid down more detailed preconditions for legal education on a state by state basis. In Saxony, for example, § 18 SächsJAPO[23] provides a list of exams students have to pass at University before they can be registered for the state examination (*Staatsexamen*).

In 2003 the traditional system was amended slightly. With the law on the reform of legal education[24] the final examination has been divided into two parts: a state examination (*Staatliche Pflichtfachprüfung*) that counts 70 % towards the final degree and a University examination (*Universitäre Schwerpunktbereichsprüfung*) that counts 30 % towards the final degree. This two-element system is the reason why the name of the examination changed from state examination (*Staatsexamen*) to first law examination (*Erste Juristische Prüfung*).

The state examination (Staatliche Pflichtfachprüfung)

The content of the state examination is regulated by each state (*Land*). Usually students have to take five to six written exams of five hours

22 Official Journal of the EC, L 327/45.

23 Ausbildungs- und Prüfungsordnung für Juristen des Freitaates Sachsen.

24 Gesetz zur Reform der Juristenausbildung vom 11.07.2002, BGBl. I p. 2592.

each. In addition to that they have to pass an oral exam.[25] In the case that a student would fail the exam he can repeat the state examination once.[26] Those students, who take the exam earlier than defined by the course of study, have the possibility to repeat it twice (*Freiversuch* = free attempt).[27] If they have passed the *Freiversuch* they may – in contrast to other students – try to improve their grade by sitting the whole examination again (*Verbesserungsversuch*).[28] The grade of this new attempt only counts if it is better than the *Freiversuch.*
One or two semesters of studies abroad do not count for the *Freiversuch.*[29] Thus those students who study abroad have no disadvantages with regard to the final examination.

The University examination

The University examination covers one special field of law (e.g. European Law, Business Law or Intellectual Property Law). The content of the exam is laid down by each University. That means that since July 2003 students have to take some sort of final examination at University. But it is not a degree in the sense of the Bologna process. With the first law examination students do not receive an academic degree at all.

25 E.g. § 28 Abs. 2 Ausbildungs- und Prüfungsordnung für Juristen - JAPO (Bavaria); §§ 23 Abs. 2, 26 Sächsische Juristenausbildungs- und Prüfungsordnung – SächsJAPO (Saxony).
26 § 5d Abs. 5 S. 1 DRiG (see Fn 21).
27 § 5d Abs. 5 S. 2 DRiG (see Fn 21), § 29 SächsJAPO.
28 E.g. § 31 Abs 1 SächsJAPO.
29 The preconditions for the Freiversuch are laid down state by state, e.g. in Saxony in § 29 SächsJAPO.

An element of Bologna in German legal education

Thus the Bologna system is not fully implemented into German legal education.

Nevertheless there are some attempts to combine the traditional system with the ideas of Bologna. Some law faculties in Germany offer a Bachelor's degree in addition to the traditional education. For example the Law Faculty of the Technische Universität Dresden offers the Bachelor programme "Law in Context – Law in an international context with regard to engineering, politics and economy"[30]. This course of study covers 6 semesters. After their Bachelor's degree students have to study for another two or four semesters to prepare for the first law examination. The advantage of this system is that students gain a first University degree after three years. Following that they can decide whether they want to go on with law by applying for a Master's degree or for the first law examination or whether they want to change to another subject. Moreover graduates can decide to start working – although in that case they are not allowed to work in the so called regulated legal professions (*reglementierte juristische Berufe*), that is to say solicitor, barrister, notary or judge. For these professions the first law examination is compulsory.

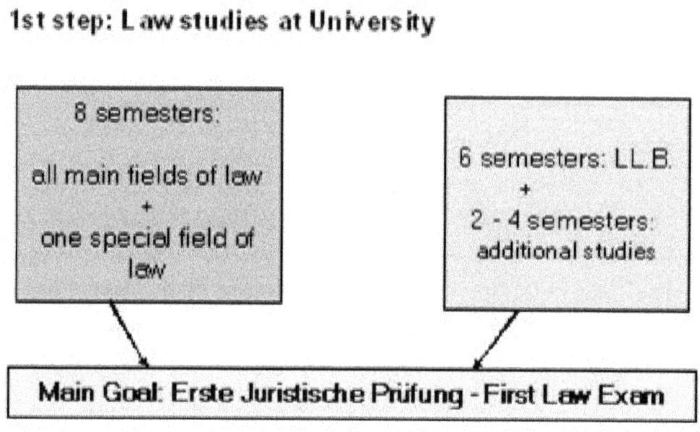

Figure 1: Law Studies at University

The main goal for students, who took the first law examination, is the admission to the legal traineeship offered by the state (*Rechtsreferendariat*).

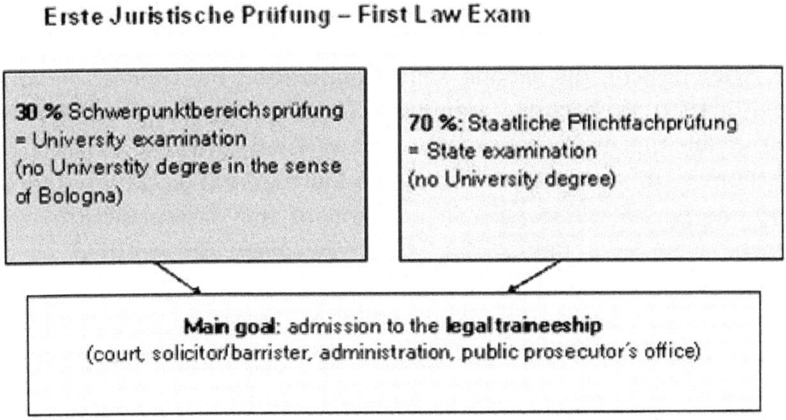

Figure 2: First Law Exam

Legal Traineeship (Rechtsreferendariat)

The traineeship is obligatory for those graduates who want to enter into the regulated legal professions. The overall content of the traineeship is again laid down by the Federal Government whereas the details are regulated state by state.

During their time as a legal trainee graduates are employed by the state as civil servants or public service employees – depending on the state (*Land*) where they spend their traineeship. The legal trainees have to pass several stages – e.g. with a law firm, at court, with a public prosecutor or in the public administration. They draft pleadings and procedural documents. Moreover they are allowed to act as public prosecutors in minor cases. The traineeship covers two years[31] and ends with the second state examination (*Zweites Staatsexamen* or *Assessorexamen*). The trainees have to pass eight to eleven written exams, depending on the law of each state (*Land*), and – again – an oral exam. Only these results count for the final grade. The results of the exams that the trainees wrote during their stages are not part of it.[32]

After passing the second state examination the trainees have the "qualification to become a judge" (*Befähigung zum Richteramt*)[33]. That means that they can practice in any legal profession except that of a notary. In some states (*Ländern*) the registration as a notary requires a special traineeship in addition to the *Referendariat*.[34] The trainees who have passed the *Assessorexamen* are entitled to call themselves "Assessor iuris" (Ass.iur.).

There is no special bar examination in Germany. Lawyers merely have to register with the bar. In this respect the *Assesorexamen* is also a bar examination. The principle behind that is the so called *Einheitsjurist*. That means that all graduates who seek access to a regulated profession are educated uniformly.

The advantage of this system is that a judge has at least some experience as a lawyer and vice versa. Thus legal education supports the mutual understanding among the legal professions. Besides that each *Assessor* is in principle able to work in any field of law.

The Grading system in Germany

The grading system in the traditional German legal education is based on a scale of 0 to 18 points. The pass mark is 4 points.

---

31 § 5b Abs. 1 DRiG (see Fn 21).

32 § 5d Abs. 4 S. 4 DRiG (see Fn 21).

33 § 5 Abs. 1 DRiG (see Fn 21).

34 E. g. for Saxony: <http://www.notarkammer-sachsen.de/notar.htm#berufsziel>, 04.12.2012.

<table>
<tr><th>German points</th><th>German grades</th><th>ECTS-grades</th></tr>
<tr><td>18</td><td rowspan="3">Sehr gut
(very good)</td><td rowspan="7">A</td></tr>
<tr><td>17</td></tr>
<tr><td>16</td></tr>
<tr><td>15</td><td rowspan="3">Gut
(good)</td></tr>
<tr><td>14</td></tr>
<tr><td>13</td></tr>
<tr><td>12</td><td rowspan="3">Voll befriedigend
(very satisfactory)</td></tr>
<tr><td>11</td><td rowspan="3">B</td></tr>
<tr><td>10</td></tr>
<tr><td>9</td><td rowspan="3">Befriedigend
(satisfactory)</td></tr>
<tr><td>8</td><td rowspan="2">C</td></tr>
<tr><td>7</td></tr>
<tr><td>6</td><td rowspan="3">Ausreichend
(sufficient)</td><td rowspan="2">D</td></tr>
<tr><td>5</td></tr>
<tr><td>4</td><td>E</td></tr>
<tr><td>3</td><td rowspan="3">Mangelhaft
(unsatisfactory)</td><td rowspan="3">FX</td></tr>
<tr><td>2</td></tr>
<tr><td>1</td></tr>
<tr><td>0</td><td>Ungenügend
(insufficient)</td><td>F</td></tr>
</table>

The scheme above gives only an example for the classification of ECTS-grades. The scale might be slightly different state by state.

The final grade of the First Law Examination and of the Second State Examination represents an average mark and is defined as follows:

German points	Final grade
14,0 – 18,0	Sehr gut (very good)
11,5 – 13,99	Gut (good)
9,0 – 11,49	Vollbefriedigend (very satisfactory)
6,5 – 8,99	Befriedigend (satisfactory)
4,0 – 6,49	Ausreichend (sufficient = pass mark)

Some of the new Bachelor programmes have changed this grading system to a scale of 0 to 5 points in order to make it more compatible with the European Master programmes. In that case students can ask for a translation into the 18-points-system if they aim for the First Law Examination.

PhD and Habilitation – academic career

Besides the regulated professions some lawyers choose an academic career.

PhD – doctoral degree

After the First Law Examination or after a Master's degree students can decide to make their PhD at a Law Faculty. Most Faculties do not offer a special PhD programme. Doctoral students may enrol as a PhD student. But this does not entail any obligation to take lectures or seminars. In principle there are no time limits for PhD students – except of some restrictions by institutions who support students by providing them financial aid.

The preconditions for a PhD are laid down by each state[35] and – on the basis of the state regulation – the details are fixed University by University. In general doctoral candidates would write their doctoral thesis in about 3 years. The final steps towards the title "Dr. iur." are the submission of the doctoral thesis and the final rigorosum or the final disputation, depending on the regulations of the law faculty where the thesis has been submitted. Doctoral candidates may call themselves "Dr. iur." after they have published their thesis.

Habilitation

Those lawyers who aim to start an academic career as a law professor at a German University have to write a habilitation thesis[36]. Besides the PhD[37] it requires the first law examination although it is common that professors have also passed the *Assessorexamen.* Moreover post-doctoral candidates have to prove profound experiences in research and teaching. Again generally speaking there are no time limits for the submission of the habilitation thesis except of some restrictions for researchers who work as assistant professors at University. Their employment is normally limited to 6 years.[38]

If the habilitation thesis is accepted by a law faculty and the candidate has passed the oral examination his official title is Dr. habil. (doctor habilitatus). He has the position of a *Privatdozent.* Only if he

---

35 E.g. § 27 SächsHG.

36 Law professors at Universities of Applied Sciences or Polytechnics are not necessarily obliged to write a habilitation thesis.

37 E.g. § 30 Abs. 1 SächsHG.

38 § 2 Abs. 1 Wissenschaftszeitvertragsgesetz (WissZVG); <http://www.gesetze-im-internet.de/bundesrecht/wisszeitvg/gesamt.pdf>, 04.12.2012.

is holding a chair at a law faculty a Doctor habilitatus is allowed to use the title *ordentlicher Professor*.

Juniorprofessor – junior professor

Since 2002 another kind of professorship has been established at German Universities: the junior professor *(Juniorprofessor)*. A *Juniorprofessor* is not necessarily doctor habilitatus. He is employed as a public service employee for 6 years at the most to gain experience as an independent researcher and lecturer earliest possible. The junior professorship was established to "provide young scientist with a new avenue towards a professorship"[39]. Due to the so called Federalism reform in Germany in 2006 the states *(Länder)* are responsible for regulations regarding junior professorships.[40]

European Lawyer – EEC lawyer

Under Directive 98/5/EC[41] a lawyer has the right to practice in another member state under the professional title of his home-country. In Germany the directive has been implemented by the *Gesetz über die Tätigkeit europäischer Rechtsanwälte in Deutschland (EuRAG[42])*. To get registered as EEC lawyer under German Law the applicant has to prove the admission to the bar in his home country.

To get the admission to the bar in Germany under the German professional title *Rechtsanwalt* EEC lawyers can choose between three different avenues:

1. If a lawyer has practiced as an established European Lawyer in Germany in the field of German law for three years without a

---

39 Federal Ministry of Education and Research; <http://www.bmbf.de/en/820.php>, 04.12.2012.

40 E.g. § 70 SächsHG.

41 Official Journal of the EC L 77/36.

42 BGBl I S. 182, 1349; <http://bundesrecht.juris.de/eurag/>, 12.11.2012.

break[43] he can apply for a registration as *Rechtsanwalt*. Lawyers have to prove their professional experience to the bar by providing them with a list of cases they have worked on.

2. If a lawyer has practiced as an established European Lawyer in Germany for three years without a focus on German Law he can apply for a registration as *Rechtsanwalt* by proving his capacity to continue practicing as a lawyer in German law.[44] The lawyer has to meet the preconditions under 1. and, in addition to that, he has to prove professional experience and practice in German law by certificates of seminars etc.[45] Besides that lawyers have to be interviewed by the bar about their work experience and their experience with German Law.[46]
3. If a European lawyer seeks the admission to the bar with less than three years of practice he has to pass an aptitude test. The test is offered by the same examination offices that are responsible for the second state examination.[47] It covers two written examinations and one oral examination.[48]

---

43 § 11 Abs. 1 EuRAG (see Fn. 42); only minor breaks of less than three weeks are accepted (§ 11 Abs. 2 EuRAG).

44 § 13 Abs. 1 EuRAG (see Fn. 42).

45 §§ 13 Abs. 2, 14 EuRAG (see Fn. 42).

46 § 15 EuRAG (see Fn. 42).

47 § 18 Abs. 1 EuRAG (see Fn. 42); that is to say the ministries of justice of the *Länder*.

48 § 21 EuRAG (see Fn. 42). The content of the examination covers civil law as a compulsory subject and the following optional subjects: 1. public law or criminal law; 2. trade law, labour law, civil law (as far as it is not covered by the compulsory subject), public law or criminal law. Details are laid down by the *Länder* (e.g. Baden-Württemberg (also valid for Saxony): <http://justizportal-bw.de/servlet/PB/show/1149111/Verordnung%20Eignungspr%FCfung.pdf>, 27.09.2010.

Conclusion

German legal education has been discussed for a long time. It seems to be a never ending story between those who want to remain faithful to the traditional system and those who want to take the opportunity, given by the Bologna process, to enforce some more reforms. Both positions are understandable and both are defended by their supporters for good reasons. But in the end the positions are not as far away from each other as often claimed. Both parties want lawyers to be well educated. Both parties see the necessity to have high quality standards. Merely the avenue to meet these standards is different. But many roads lead to Rome. Thus it seems to be more a question of quality management than of a decision between Bachelor and *Staatsexamen.* Of course, the devil is in the details but it is worth working towards a solution that meets the Bologna requirements as well as the – undoubtedly high quality – traditional education standards in Germany.

How to become a lawyer in Italy

Gianmaria AJANI

Legal Education

To be qualified as lawyer (*avvocato*) in Italy, the law sets three main requirements:

1. To be holder of a law degree *(laurea magistrale in Giurisprudenza)*;
2. To have practiced as an intern with a law firm for at least 18 months;
3. To have passed with success the Bar exam.

The law degree is delivered by a Law School *(Dipartimento di Giurisprudenza)*, an academic institution (either public or private) recognised by the Ministry of Higher Education, after having attended 5 years of University training. The law degree is delivered to students having accomplished a curriculum composed of 30 exams, for a total of 300 credits (60 credits per year), and having defended a thesis before a panel of professors from his/her Department.

Unlike most part of University Departments, Law Departments in Italy have abandoned the Bologna framework, the so called "3 + 2" scheme. The *laurea magistrale in giurisprudenza*, therefore, represents the only degree that is taken by students interested in becoming lawyers.

Quite similarly to what happens in continental Europe, Italian Law Schools do not train only students interested in the legal practice. On average, less than 30% of all graduated per year do apply, later on, for the Bar exam. A minimal number of graduates opts for other forensic careers, like the Judiciary and the Notariat.

A large amount of graduates spends the degree in law in other, more or less related fields, like in-house consultants, public officials, managers in public and private institutions, and the like. This explains why the curriculum of courses taken during the 5 years includes subjects that are not purely forensic, or related to the legal practice, such as: history of law, roman law, comparative law, macroeconomics, legal philosophy. These course, together with the more practical oriented subjects, like private law, criminal law, civil and criminal procedure, tax law, administrative law, are generally compulsory, even if the retaking of failed exams is possible.

There is no limited access to be enrolled as law student; the only requirement to be admitted is to have received a degree from a high school (5 years of education). Usually, therefore, 1st year law students are 18-19 years old.

Legal Practice: internship and Bar exam

Internship in a law firm is a requested pre-requisite to be admitted to the Bar exam.

Recently (2012) the 24-month length of the internships has been reduced to 18 months, and 6 of them can be employed even before the completion of the law degree. An intern can be authorised to mature part of his/her practice in a foreign law firm, while a foreign national who has received a law degree from a non Italian University can be admitted as an intern upon evaluation of his/her degree and of his/her actual knowledge of Italian law by the competent Bar council.

Once the intern *(praticante)* has finished the practice, he/she is ready to apply for the admittance to the Bar.

Bar exam

Admittance to the Bar is governed through a nation wide selection, that occurs on a yearly basis. Every year, in December, applicants have to sustain a written proof based on three different tests: an opinion on private law, an opinion on criminal law, and the preparation of a legal deed (such as a claim, or a request for injunction). While the exam is held nation wide-on a set of identical cases, the selecting committee sits in every legal District (a District being the territory where a Court of Appeal has jurisdiction). Applicants sustain the tests at the District where they are registered as interns, before a committee composed of two lawyers, two law professors and two judges.

After 5/6 months the results of the written tests are published, and applicant who have received a positive evaluation on the 3 proofs are called to sustain the oral exam. The latter is based on a range of 6 matters (such as private, commercial, labour, International law, criminal and civil procedure, deontology). While the choice of the matters is left to every candidate, procedural matters and deontology are compulsory matters. After a successful examination, a candidate is admitted to the Bar, attached to the District where he or she has passed the exams.

Intra EU practice

EU citizens, holding a law degree delivered within the European Law are not automatically admitted to the Bar. To be recognised as Italian lawyer, the interested person has to follow a procedure of recognition, governed by Decree no. 206/2007, implementing EU Directive 2005/36. According to the said regulation, a foreign lawyer willing to practice within the Italian jurisdiction has to go through a test aimed to assess his/her capability to practice in the country. The matter remains somehow controversial, as according to some commentators the mentioned test does not fully respect EU regulation on the free movement of professionals.

The professional and vocational training of lawyers according to the Anglo-Saxon model in a mixed legal system – The case of the Republic of Mauritius

Rajendra Parsad GUNPUTH

Introduction

How is the vocational training of lawyers done in Mauritius whose legal system is a mixed one consisting of both the common law and most of the romano-germanic laws? Above all, in the aftermath of its independence in 1968, Mauritius inherited a written Constitution[49] which provides for the possibility of an appeal before the Judicial Committee of the Privy Council[50], but under very strict conditions[51]. Nevertheless, there are innumerable questions which arise concerning the exercise of this legal profession in a mixed legal system: how do these aboriginals adapt to these laws, and how are the latter interpreted?

First of all, the history of Mauritius' double colonization must be understood. Conquered by France in 1715, and then by Great Britain from 1715 to 1810, «*l'Isle de France*» became Mauritius and gained its independence on the 12th March 1968. It inherited both the French and English law, with the consequence of a juridical blend, which nonetheless remains difficult to manage and/or to intepret.

49 Text which is written by the Professor Stanley de Smith of University of Cambridge. This English version is translated by the Professor Louis Favoreau of University of Aix-de-Provence, Marseille.

50 Section 81 of the Constitution 1968.

51 Provided the Supreme Court of Mauritius has so authorized or with leave of the Supreme Court.

In fact, the Capitulation Act 1810 (l'*Acte de Capitulation*), issued by her Gracious Majesty, Queen Elizabeth II, clearly states that the inhabitants of the island will preserve their laws, customs and religions. From 1715 to 1810, *l'Isle de France* inherited several codes including the Code Napoléon 1804, the Code de Commerce 1807 and the French Penal Code 1789[52]. Known for its great promptness, several UK-inspired laws have emerged throughout the years and this explains why the judicial system of Mauritius looks forward to judgments of the *Cour de cassation* and the UK House of Lords. The local judgments are then compiled in the Mauritius Reports (MR) or Supreme Court Judgment (SCJ). Actually, all these foreign laws, together with the overseas decisions, are important juridical tools for those who practise in the legal profession.

There are very few avenues concerning the general organization of legal studies in Mauritius. In fact, potential barristers have very few options: either they go to UK (England or Wales) to follow this vocational training or they secure a seat at the University of Mauritius since the promulgation of the *Law Practitioner's Act 1984*. Only this law regulates the recognition of degrees obtained either in England, Wales or in Mauritius and the exercise of this liberal profession in Mauritius. There have been several major reforms which must be studied.

In order to understand the professional organization of lawyers in Mauritius better, several possibilities will arise, namely: access to law studies in Mauritius on the one hand, and the difficulties encountered when gaining access to the training of barristers on the other hand.

---

52 There are two kinds of codification in Mauritian law: a formal codification, according to the French model, with codes, and a real codification, according to the English model, with laws which have been chronologically compiled in statutory books.

Access to law studies

First of all, how do future potential lawyers obtain access to legal studies? Throughout the years, Mauritius, unlike other African countries, has built a solid and dynamic judicial system with courts based on the Anglo-Saxon model[53]. Nevertheless, the Supreme Court of Mauritius remains the highest local jurisdiction with unlimited jurisdiction[54].

Since Mauritius wanted to become one of the pillars of the Indian Ocean, be it in the economic, financial or political area, and given the recent development in the various sectors (the banking sector, financial sector, offshore companies) with the hope of becoming as powerful as Singapore, Mauritius' need for lawyers proved to be more and more pressing.

It is in this view that the Department of Law at the University of Mauritius was set up (established under the *University of Mauritius Act 1971*) to offer law courses. However, since the number of seats at the University of Mauritius were limited and were allocated in a selective manner, most of the Mauritian students, after having completed their baccalaureate or Higher School Certificate (HSC), opted to study abroad in prestigious French and English Universities, given the fact that they master the English as well as the French language.

After having taken oath[55] before various Inns of Court (Gray's Inn, Inner Temple, Lincoln's Inn, Middle Temple), the Mauritian youth returned to the island where they could practise before the local tribunals after following a pupillage in a lawyer's Chamber. On the other hand, the notary's and attorney's profession did not require any law degree or training whatsoever. Mostly clerks, after long years of practice, became notaries or attorneys (*as per* their choice) until the

53 With District Courts, intermediate Court, court of Assizes, Industrial Court just to name a few.

54 Section 76 of the Constitution 1968.

55 Mauritians who are solicitors or notaries and who took their examinations in England, Wales or elsewhere cannot practice in Mauritius. Only Mauritians who did their bar in England may practice in Mauritius.

Council of Legal Education (CLE) cropped up and the latter imposed law examinations for potential barristers, notaries and attorneys.

TRAINING	SUBJECTS PROVIDED BY THE COUNCIL OF LEGAL EDUCATION OF THE SUPREME COURT OF MAURITIUS
BARRISTER	Evidence, Famille, Civil Procedure, Criminal Procedure, Administrative Law, Constitutional Law, Droit du travail, Company Law, Statutory Interpretation, Criminal Law, les Obligations, Effets de Commerce, Droit des Affaires
ATTORNEY	Civil Procedure, Sûretés, Administrative law, Constitutional Law, Criminal Law, Company Law, Statutory Interpretation, Les Obligations, Land Acquisition Act 1973, Effets de Commerce, Droit des Affaires
NOTARY	Legal Drafting, Successions, Famille, Vente, Biens

Table no. 1

From the outset, the lawyers', notaries' or attorneys' profession will be regulated by *the Law Practitioners Act 1984*. The Mauritian students would then have two principal choices: either they go to UK or Wales to complete their LLB and be sworn before the various Inns of Court (*supra*), or they complete their Bachelor of Laws (LLB (Hons)) at the University of Mauritius. The second choice applies mostly to those students who have financial constraints.

UNIVERSITIES	THE SUBJECTS TAUGHT	DURATION	DEGREES ISSUED
UNIVERSITY OF MAURITIUS	Droit civil, Droit administratif, Droit constitutionnel, Revenue Law, Taxation Law, Law of Trusts, Philosophie du droit amongst others	3 years (full-time) or 4 years (part-time)	LLB (Hons)
UNIVERSITIES IN ENGLAND AND WALES	Advocacy, Civil Procedure, Administrative Law, Constitutional Law, Family Law, Revenue Law, Law of Trusts amongst others	3 years (full-time) or 4 years (part-time)	LLB (Hons)
FRENCH UNIVERSITIES	Droit civil, Droit social, Droit Administratif, Droit Constitutionnel, Histoire du Droit, Régimes Matrimoniaux, les Successions, Droit des Affaires, Informatique juridique, amongst others	3 years (full-time) or 4 years (part-time)	Licence de Droit (private or public as applicable)

Table no. 2

The courses offered by the University of Mauritius are normally delivered by local academics (see Table 2) who already have a law degree and who lecture well both in English and French (see Table 3). Most of them have a *"Licence de Droit"* or *"Maîtrise de Droit"* from French universities but nothing prevents a holder of a Bachelor in Law (LLB (Hons)) or a Master in Law from English universities or the University of Mauritius to lecture as well. However, it must be noted that foreign academics can also teach law in Mauritius on a contractual basis, for a period of 2 years, with the possibility of renewal.

LAW	SUBJECTS	APPLICATIONS
FRENCH CIVIL LAW	Droit de la famille, droit des personnes, droit de la vente et les contrats spéciaux, droit des obligations, droits des successions, droit des régimes matrimoniaux, droit du travail, droit pénal français (except for Conspiracy)	Application of French civil law but the procedure is English-based with the Divorce and Judicial Separation Act 1982, Successions and Wills Act 1883, Landlord and Tenant Act 1999 as well as injunctions
ENGLISH LAW	Judicial Review or *Droit Administratif*, Human Rights or *Droit de l'Homme*, Revenue Law, Taxation Law, Company Law, Good Governance, Alternative Dispute Resolution (ADR)	Application of English law without relying on the English procedure (*habeas corpus*, arrest and seizure, warrants, fundamental rights of the citizens) since the laws are of English origin: Criminal Procedure Act 1853, Criminal Appeal Act 1955
LAW OTHER THAN THE FRENCH CIVIL LAW OR ENGLISH LAW	Company Law (New Zealand), Prevention of Corruption Act 2002 (Singapore), Prevention of Terrorism Act 2002 (Hong Kong)	Application of the law of New Zealand, Singapore and Hong Kong

Table no. 3

It is in this optic that a Memorandum of Understanding was signed between the University of Aix-en-Provence and the University of Mauritius. This cooperation demanded several years of collaboration so that, first of all, the Mauritian students could master perfectly the French civil law, and then so that the university of Mauritius could, in the meantime, broaden its collaboration with other renowned French universities.

The difficulty in accessing the training for lawyers

Without being pessimistic, the potential lawyers/barristers will face hurdles of all kinds. First of all, the Mauritian students who cannot afford to go to UK or Wales, are left with only one choice: to get selected and secure a seat at the University of Mauritius, given that there is a high demand for this course coupled with the fact that only the best students would be selected. On the other hand, certain British universities, except the most prestigious ones, are more lenient where selections of students are concerned, and consequently, students with average or even below average results are admitted (see diagram below).

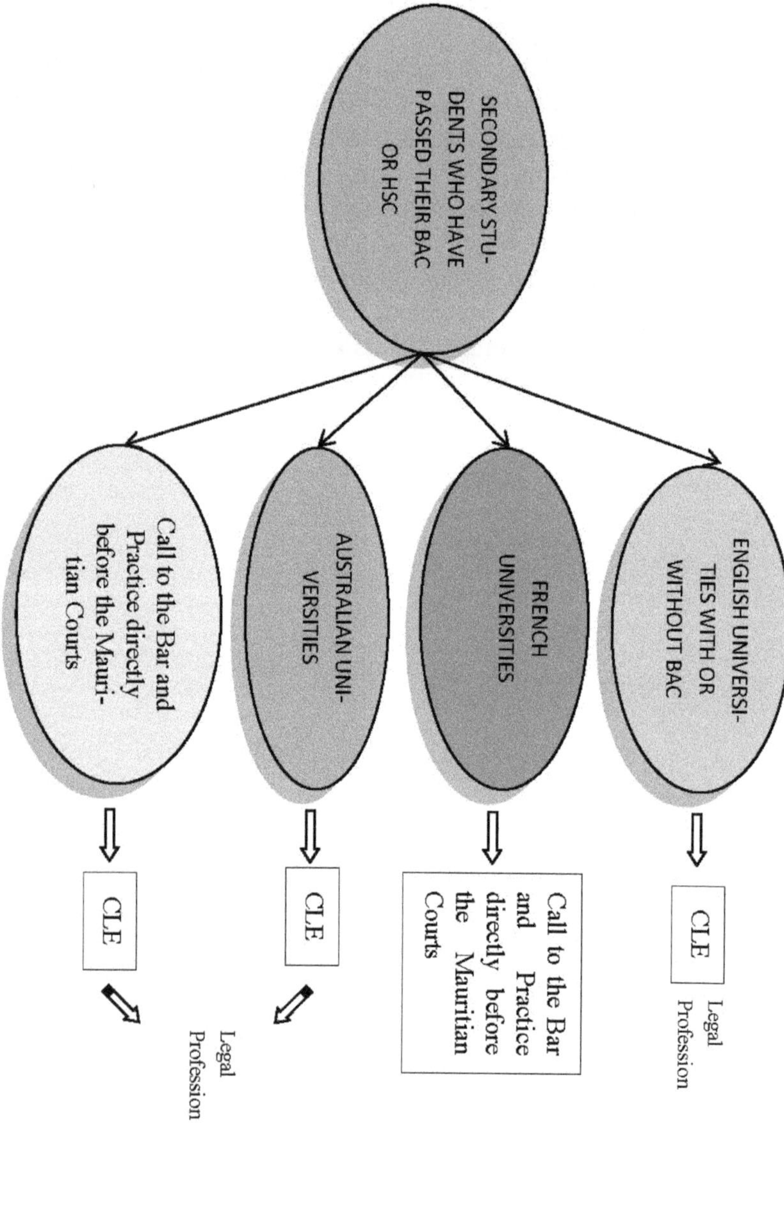
SECONDARY STU-
DENTS WHO HAVE
PASSED THEIR BAC
OR HSC
ENGLISH UNIVERSI-
TIES WITH OR
WITHOUT BAC
CLE
Legal
Profession
FRENCH
UNIVERSITIES
Call to the Bar and Practice directly before the Mauritian Courts
AUSTRALIAN UNI-
VERSITIES
CLE
Legal
Profession
Call to the Bar and
Practice directly
before the Mauri-
tian Courts
CLE

Nevertheless, UK universities allow non-law students to follow a conversion course but they should at least hold a degree and it does not matter whether it is in Mathematics, Physics or Chemistry. These students will follow a one-year course (full time in UK) or one and a half years (part time and distance learning) or two years (part time in UK) with some law subjects which will allow them to be the bearer of a Post Graduate Diploma in Law (PGDLaw) which will open the door to the Bar Council in England and to practise as a lawyer in Mauritius! However, students from the University of Mauritius see this windfall of a very average eye. They believe that they follow more thorough courses with an increased selection for three years while other Mauritian students who hold a PGDLaw (*supra*) have it the easier way! Furthermore, they have to pass the exams of the Council of Legal Education with minimal chances to succeed 9the rate of success is very low (see Table 5).

On the other hand, the Mauritian students who have passed the law degree from a French University cannot take part in the examinations of the Council of Legal Education unless they have at least a Masters of Law from a French University with a minimum pass (*Mention Assez Bien* or their application failed) grade (See Table 4)!

Universities	Selection Criteria and Qualifications	Admitted/ Rejected
UNIVERSITY OF MAURITIUS	Higher School Certificate from Cambridge University and only students with 5 As	Admitted
UK UNIVERSITIES	Higher School Certificate from Cambridge University but Mauritian students can get a place with low or even mediocre results. If they hold a degree, they can pass the conversion course and leave with a Post Graduate Diploma in Law and then be a member of one of the Inns of Court.	Admitted
FRENCH UNIVERSITIES	Higher School Certificate of Cambridge University but Mauritian students cannot have a place with low or even mediocre results.	Rejected

Table no. 4

Furthermore, Mauritian students having completed their studies at the University of Mauritius and having received their degree of Bachelor of Laws (LLB (Hons)), can now take part in the examination set up by the Council of Legal Education and which remained under the aegis of the judiciary since its creation in 1984. The courses are dispensed by the law practitioners (attorneys, barristers, magistrates and judges of the Supreme Court of Mauritius). However, in 2013 and onwards, the University of Mauritius, with the support of the Minister of Justice (Attorney General of Mauritius), will welcome the would-be barristers, attorneys and notaries. The University of Mauritius will provide infrastructures, lectures, venues and conduct examinations.

The Law Practitioners (Amendment) Act 2011 is an Act of Parliament aiming to bring underlying and important reforms to the *Law Practitioners Act 1984.* The new law, freshly amended, will however only come in force in September 2012. Henceforth, the Mauritian student who has been called to the Bar in England, Wales, France, the United States or any other Commonwealth[56] country can practice as a lawyer in Mauritius[57].

The shifting of the *Council of Legal Education*, which will become the *Council for Vocational Legal Education* after the amendment of the *Law Practitioners Act 1984*, from the hands of the judiciary to those of the University of Mauritius deserves some explanation: pass rate very very low, inappropriate pedagogical courses, lack of premises and funds, social injustice amongst others (see Table 5).

Another law which make lawyers cringe is surely *The Institute of Judicial and Legal Studies Act*[58]. It imposes that lawyers and magistrates have to follow law courses to improve themselves in their workplace[59].

---

56 Section 3 of the Law Practitioner's (Amendment) Act 2011:
"Law degree means a degree in law awarded, following a full time course of studies for such period and at such level as may be prescribed under section 22(1) (c). by: (a) the University of Mauritius; (b) a university in the United Kingdom; or (c) such university or other tertiary education institution in Mauritius, the United States, another Commonwealth country or a civil State, as may be approved by the Council."

57 Section 3 of the Law Practitioner's (Amendment) Act 2011:
"Professional qualification means an attestation, in such form as the Council may approve, to the effect that a person who holds a law degree has a qualification as, or equivalent to that of barrister entitling him to practise in: (a) England and Wales, or such other Commonwealth country as may be prescribed; or (b) the United States."

58 It is the Institute for Judicial and Legal Studies Act 2011, Act No. 26 of 2011.

59 Section 5 of the Institute for Judicial and Legal Studies Act 2011:
"The institute shall have such functions as are necessary or expedient to further its objects most effectively and shall, in particular- (a) conduct or supervise courses, seminars or workshops for the continuing training of judicial and legal officers; (b) devise, organize and conduct Continuing Professional Development Programmes for law practitioners, including legal officers, and courses for prospective judicial and legal officers and law practitioners who qualified as such in a State other than Mauritius…"

EXAMI-NATIONS	NUMBER	NUMBER OF PASSES	%
BARRISTER	60-65	1 and maximum 3 or 4	1-7%
ATTORNEY	30-32	Zero admitted or 1 or a maximum of 2/3	3.3-10%
NOTARY	10-12	Zero admitted or only 1	0-10%
TOTAL	100-109		

Table no. 5

The subjects taught at the *Council of Legal Education* are purely pedagogical while the candidates thought the courses will be more practical. The table below (Table 6) gives a list of courses undertaken by the *Council of Legal Education.*

COUNCIL OF LEGAL EDUCATION OF THE SUPREME COURT OF MAURITIUS: LIST OF SUBJECTS FOR THE BARRISTER EXAMINATION	
PAPER	SUBJECTS
PAPER 1	Evidence
PAPER 2	Civil Procedure
PAPER 3	Criminal Procedure

Table no. 6a

PAPER 4	Constitutional Law and Administrative Law	60%
PAPER 5	Criminal Law, Statutory Interpretation and Company Law	60%
PAPER 6	Civil Law: Famille, Biens, Travail, Obligations	60%
PAPER 7	ADVOCACY	60%

Table no. 6b

The second schedule of the *Law Practitioner's (Amendment) Act 2011* makes provision for new subjects (See Table 7).

PROFESSI-ON	SUBJECTS
BARRISTER	Conferencing, Drafting of legal documents, Ethics and Opinion Writing
BARRISTER AND ATTORNEY	Administrative and Constitutional Law, Advocacy, Arbitration and Mediation, Civil Procedure, Criminal Procedure, Dispute Resolution, Evidence
NOTARY	Civil Procedure, Commercial and Business Law, Practical aspects of family law, practical aspects of the law of immovable property, *"Rédaction des Actes"*, Revenue and Taxation Law, *"Tenue de l'office notarial"*

Table no. 7

Before moving on, it is worth noting concerning the sources of law that Mauritian law has been inspired from foreign laws, principally those from the UK but never hesitates in taking laws which can be put into domestic law in its own hierarchy of norms and this due to a transposition of norms which introduces foreign laws, including the international conventions[60], just like bills in the Mauritian parliament which then become Acts of Parliament after a series of lectures until they are assented by the President of the Republic of Mauritius and promulgated in the Government Gazette.

Here a question arises: the students who have the British training, meaning those who went to the UK or Wales and who are now back in the country, have not had the opportunity to learn French law while the students from French universities have not had the opportunity to learn English law and as already mentioned, Mauritius has a mixed system of law. But then, it has been demonstrated that the transposi-

60 For example the 4 Geneva Conventions 1949 which take the form of the Geneva Convention Act 2003.

tion of juridical concepts originating from another legal system is it only a translation or an adaptation[61]?

Around thirty young lawyers return to the country annually and have trouble making a place for themselves because of the ferocious competition, premises are too expensive or rare, customers are being scarcer and all papers and administrative documents are centralized in Port Louis, the capital, only. In addition to that, some Mauritian students who have passed the exams of the Council of Legal Education and come to swell an already saturated profession.

The young lawyers, freshly landed, have difficulties to survive except if they are employed by the State Law Office to practise as State Law Officers, Senior State Law Officers, Parliamentary Counsel, Solicitor General and from there they can intend to become a magistrate of a district court (there are nine of them) and which are spread across the Mauritian territory including that of Rodrigues, but they should have at least 2 years experience of practice before a court of law and then they have the opportunity to be promoted to magistrate of the Intermediate court, Registrar of the Supreme Court, Director of Public Prosecutions, while to become Judges[62] of the Supreme Court, which is the highest jurisdiction in Mauritius, a minimum of 5 years experience is required from the profession of ex magistrate, Registrar of the Supreme Court, Parliamentary counsel amongst others.

If the majority of local Magistrates have followed this step before being promoted to the supreme post, their nomination, on the other hand, is regulated by the Judicial and Legal Service Commission and

61 Pr. Stéphanie Dijoux: *La transposition des concepts juridiques originaux dans un autre système de droit: traduction ou adaptation?*

62 According to section 77(1) of the Constitution:
"1.The Chief Justice shall be appointed by the President acting after consultation with the Prime Minister. 2.The Senior Puisne Judge shall be appointed by the President, acting in accordance with the advice of the Chief Justice. 3. The Puisne Judges shall be appointed by the President, acting in accordance with the advice of the Judicial and Legal Service Commission. 4. No person shall be qualified for appointment as a Judge of the Supreme Court unless he is, and has been for at least 5 years, a barrister entitled to practise before the Supreme Court..."

the Constitution[63], supreme law of the land, which gives the Supreme Court[64] its powers.

The only small regret is that the choice of the Magistrates or Judges is done among the lawyers of the State Law Office and never among those practising in the private or academics of the University of Mauritius. This very small and hermetic circle is often condemned but a solution to this persistent loophole will be found in due time.

Conclusion

Without being pessimist, young law professionals are finding it harder to find a place for them in this tropical island and consequently, the heavenly dreams of some are fading away like snow in broad sunlight and which explains the escape of the great local minds to foreign countries like Canada, France, UK and the USA principally. Numerous Mauritian lawyers have opened their doors to the big foreign cabinets notably Anglo-Saxon. They can, however, find employment in the offshore companies which are mushrooming very quickly in the capital and also in the Cyber City Ebène, which very near to the University of Mauritius. With the double taxation avoidance agreement between Mauritius and several countries, including India, numerous Indian companies would prefer to employ young local lawyers. The Judicial Committee of the Privy Council is not spared either. Instead of going to London, the Mauritian lawyers can defend their clients' interests in Mauritius itself and the case will be heard in Mauritius.

63 Section 77 of the 1968 Constitution: Nominations of Judges of the Supreme Court.

64 Section 76 of the 1968 Constitution (The Supreme Court):
"1.The Supreme Court of Mauritius is vested with general jurisdiction to hear and determine any civil or criminal proceedings under any non-disciplinary law. It is generally vested with jurisdiction and powers conferred upon it by the Constitution or any other law. 2.Subject to the provisions of article 77, the Judges of the Supreme Court are the Chief Justice, the Senior Puisne Judge and such number of Puisne Judges prescribed by the Parliament: It being heard that the burden of a judge in exercise cannot be suppressed unless the judge gives his consent."

This judicial revolution enabled lawyers to be more serene and confident in anticipation of the future which awaits them.

How to become a lawyer in Poland?

Izabela KRAŚNICKA, Izabela SKOMERSKA-MUCHOWSKA

Introduction

Legal studies have been one of the most popular majors chosen by the Polish high school graduates for many years. Graduating from a Faculty of Law has guaranteed not only a prestigious education but also variety of possibilities on the job market. Procedure to become a practicing lawyer in Poland has recently gone under several import ant reforms and access to the profession is now more state regulated and therefore open to the wider group of candidates.

Secondary education in Poland (high schools), ends with the maturity examination (so called "matura" exam – standardized national secondary school achievement examination). It is the final exam required for graduation. The maturity certificate is the graduation certificate and consists results of particular tests taken during the examination.[65] Candidates then send those results to the Law Faculties of their choice. Naturally the better results, the better chances for entering a well-ranked Law Faculty.

Legal studies are based on a five-year uniform program. Graduates from high school apply directly to the chosen Faculties of Law. There are two types of law schools in Poland:

---

65 More on the Polish educational system see: The system of education in Poland, EURYDICE, Warsaw 2008, available at: <http://www.eurydice.org.pl/files/the_system_2008.pdf> or J. Jung-Miklaszewska: The system of education in the Republic of Poland. Schools and Diplomas, Bureau for Academic Recognition and International Exchange, Warsaw 2003, available at: <http://www.buwiwm.edu.pl/publ/edu/System.pdf>.

first group includes Law Faculties at state universities (total of 17 as of October 2010), second group includes private schools which opened law major within their educational offer (there are 17 of those as well in October 2010).

Legal studies are based on a five-year uniform program as they departed from the stage-oriented propos al of the Bologna Process. Based on the guidelines prepared by the Ministry of Science and Higher Education, each Faculty designs its own curriculum for the legal studies program. It is mostly focused on the theoretical aspects of law and understanding of mechanisms functioning in the different legal disciplines.[66] During the last year of law school, students attend master seminars, where under supervision of law professors, they prepare the final master thesis. The defense of the master thesis exam is the final requirement for the law school graduation. Law studies are usually offered in the stationary (week-day) system and non-stationary (weekend sessions) system. Stationary studies are free, non-stationary students pay semester tuition.

Law school graduates obtain master of law degree and are not licensed to practice in any profession. Depending on the professional plans, lawyers-to-be may choose five different paths of further training: advocate apprenticeship, legal adviser apprenticeship[67], judge apprenticeship, prosecutor apprenticeship or public notary apprenticeship. Each apprenticeship has a different course of training and aims at providing participants with practical aspects of the legal profession. There are entrance exams to all five apprenticeship programs and final exams after successful completion of each program. Positive results in the final exams guarantee license to practice.

66 More on the content and methods of legal studies in Poland: I. Kraśnicka: Legal Education and Clinical Legal Education in Poland, International Journal of Clinical Legal Education, December 2008, pp. 48-55.

67 The division of the profession into advocates and legal advisers is of a histrocial background. At the moment the only difference is the prohibition of legal advisers to represent clients in the course of criminal proceedings.

Becoming an advocate/legal advisor

The Law on Advocacy of May 26, 1982 (with many further amendments) regulates the profession of advocates the Law on Legal Advisors of July 6, 1982 (also amended several times) applies to the profession of legal advisors. Representatives of both professions have the right to represent clients in courts. Why two groups? The division is a historical remaining of the old system. Advocates have been present in the Polish legal system for a long time, in fact first mentioning of legal representation dates back to the days of the first Polish King – Boleslaw Chrobry.[68] The profession developed dynamically and has been the core on the Polish legal system. Under the communist regime however, a new profession was established by the state authorities to provide assistance and legal representation to the state-owned enterprises and stet-oriented legal procedures. Advocates were pushed to the back of the professional possibilities and legal advisors took the floor for some time. After the transformation period both professions have been given new regulations and both have ever since been equally entitled to provide their services. Both professions have their own bar associations – one on national and several on regional levels. The only difference in the scope of representation is that legal advisors are not entitled to represent the accused in the course of criminal proceedings.

Admission to both professions, as well as the apprenticeship requirements and programs are quite similar. Entrance exams consist of 150 multiple choice questions concerning criminal, civil, business, labor, administrative, constitutional, EU law, etc. The exam leads to a three-year apprenticeship program filled with courses, seminars, workshops on different aspects of the profession. Throughout the entire program each participant of the apprenticeship has his/her own supervisor called "patron" – a licenced lawyer who is willing to mentor his/her younger colleague. Apprenticeship programs are paid pro-

68 For more information see: A. Redzik, *Szkic o dziejach adwokatury polskiej*, "Palestra" 2008, nr. 11-12, pp. 13-21.

grams – there is an annual tuition obligatory for all participants. The apprenticeship training's final stage is the licence exam which consists of different parts: mutliple choice test, essay questions, legal documents writing, etc. Positive result in the exam guarantees the licence to practice as an advocate or legal advisor.

Foreign lawyers wishing to practice in Poland are subject to the national regulation: Law on the legal assistance provided by foreign lawyers in the Republic of Poland.[69]

Becoming a judge or prosecutor

The path to become a judge or prosecutor in Poland has been modified recently in a quite significant way so it is worth to give it some special attnetion in the paragraphs below with special emphasis on judicial training.

The reform of judicial training in Poland - Background of reform

The reform of judicial training in Poland was part of the reform of Polish judicial system started in 1990's. Whole process was highly influenced by standards worked out within the framework of European organizations especially the European Union[70] and the Council of Europe. Documents of the Council of Europe were widely quoted in the governmental project of the statute on the Polish National School of the Judiciary and Public Prosecution[71]. The Government outlined the need of providing high quality of training not only from substan-

---

69 Ustawa o świadczeniu przez prawników zagranicznych pomocy prawnej w Rzeczypospolitej Polskiej, Dz. U. 2002, nr 126, poz. 1069.

70 Reform of judicial system was condition of membership of Poland in the European Union (according to so called Copenhagen criteria and subject of evaluation made by the Commission.

71 Druk sejmowy 946, p.5.

tive point of view, but also guarantying future independence and impartiality of judges.

Opinion no 4 of the Consultative Council of European Judges (CCJE) to the attention of the Committee of Ministers of the Council of Europe on appropriate initial and in-service training for judges at national and European levels

1. It is essential that judges, selected after having done full legal studies, receive detailed, in-depth, diversified training so that they are able to perform their duties satisfactorily.
2. Such training is also a guarantee of their independence and impartiality, in accordance with the requirements of the Convention for the Protection of Human Rights and Fundamental Freedoms.
3. Lastly, training is a prerequisite if the judiciary is to be respected and worthy of respect. The trust citizens place in the judicial system will be strengthened if judges have a depth and diversity of knowledge which extend beyond the technical field of law to areas of important social concern, as well as courtroom and personal skills and understanding enabling them to manage cases and deal with all persons involved appropriately and sensitively. Training is in short essential for the objective, impartial and competent performance of judicial functions, and to protect judges from inappropriate influences.

The next reason of the reform was the judgment of Polish Constitutional Court, which recognized judges' training system unconstitutional[72]. Till 2009 candidates for judges had to complete judicial training, pass final exam and work as assistant judge for prescribed period

72 Judgment of 24th October 2007, SK 7/06.

of time. The institution of the assistant judge served to prepare a person to assume the office of the judge by way of enabling the persons to gain practical experience. A statute precisely specified the requirements for the assumption of the office of an assistant judge. The office of the assistant judge may be assumed by a person holding Polish citizenship, enjoying full civil rights, having impeccable character, who has competed legal studies in Poland and has obtained a Master's degree or has completed such studies abroad, provided that the studies are recognised in Poland, who is able, regarding the person's state of health, to perform the duties of the judge, and who has also completed a judge's or a public prosecutor's traineeship and has passed a judge's or a public prosecutor's examination. Assistant judges performed two types of tasks: one within the scope of the administration of justice and the other within the scope of legal protection. Assistant judges were, while adjudicating, be independent and subject only to the Constitution and statues For the period of performing the duties of the judge an assistant judge remained under the supervision of a judge who performed the function of a consulting judge who assisted the assistant judge with judicial technique and the performance of duties related to judicial administration, as well as carries out reviews of court sessions presided over by the assistant judge. In turn, vesting the performance of judicial acts in the assistant judge lied within the competence of the Minister of Justice.

This system was challenged before the Constitutional Court. The initiators alleged non-conformity of this regulation to the Constitution, pointing to the equality between assistant judges and judges in terms of the power to adjudicate, while, simultaneously depriving assistant judges of the constitutional guarantee of independence. The Constitutional Court stated that:

1. "A statutory regulation, pursuant to which the assistant judge, while adjudicating, is independent and subject only to the Constitution and statutes, constitutes merely a declaration, which does not provide for an actual and effective independence required by the Constitution. Such a regulation needs to be accompanied by specific legal solutions with regard to the practical assurance of the observance of individual constituents making up the notion of

independence. In particular, the following are impermissible: dependence of the assistant judge on the Minister of Justice, lack of specification of the time frame as regards the assistant judge's performance of the function of the judge, exclusion of the National Council of the Judiciary from participation in the procedure of vesting in the assistant judge the performance of the duties of the judge, dependence on a regional court's board of judges and on the consulting judge, lack of guarantees as regards the political neutrality of assistant judges."[73]

2. Another reason of the reform of judicial training was ineffectiveness of former system, which was decentralized, expensive and incompatible with staff needs of courts. As a consequence in 2007 there were 1659 judicial trainees in 23 training centers. In the same year 1515 trainees had completed their judicial traineeship and passed judicial exam and only 396 of them were appointed as assistant judges.

The Polish National School of Judiciary and Public Prosecution

In 2009 the centralized system of judicial training was introduced in Poland.

The main element of the system is the Polish National School of Judiciary and Public Prosecution (The National School). The National School was established on the basis of the Act of 1st July 2005, amended by the Act of 23rd January 2009[74], commenced its operations on 1st September 2006. The School is legal person subordinate to the Minister of Justice. The tasks of the National School mainly include:

– preparing programmes of seminars and practical training for court and prosecutor trainees and undertaking organizational measures related to the implementation of the programmes in question, in-

73 English summary of the judgment <http://www.trybunal.gov.pl/eng/summaries/documents/SK_7_06_GB.pdf>.

74 Dz.U. 2009 nr 26, poz. 157.

cluding court or prosecutor specialization in frames of the ongoing training;
- providing initial training (application): general application, judge's application and prosecutor's application;
- preparing an organizing programmes of applications;
- preparing programmes of legal trainings for judge's assistants and court referendaries;
- preparing and organizing exams for judges and prosecutors;
- preparing programmes and organizing central training and other cyclical forms of professional development;
- coordinating training activities of courts and public prosecutor's offices;
- preparing and organizing conferences, symposiums, seminars related to the particular areas of law;
- international cooperation and cooperation with the faculties of law of universities, institutions and research centers with respect to the training activity and other forms of professional development;
- publishing activity related to the publication of training materials;
- other tasks related to the development of officials of common courts of law and the public prosecutor's office, designated by the Minister of Justice.

The actvivity National School includes both judge's and prosecutor's trainingship and other training activities which are mainly performed by means of seminars, conferences, symposiums, workshops and publishing activity, planned in accordance with the annual schedules prepared on the basis of the analysis of training needs reported by courts. Substantive supervision on post-graduate legal training is performed by the Minister of Justice. Bodies of the National School comprise the Programme Board and the Director. The Programme Board is composed of judges and prosecutors, persons with an academic title of professor or assistant professor in law, and judges and prosecutors emeritus. Members are appointed by Polish judicial authorities and professional self-governments. The Board is responsible i.a. for outlining general directions of activity for the National School, drafting annual schedules of training activities for the Polish National School. The Director of the National School is appointed by the Minister of Justice for a 5-year term, acting with the advice of the National Justice Board and the Board of Prosecutors at the General Prosecutor's Office.

Post-graduate legal training

General training

Recruitment for the general training scheme is conducted in the form of a 2-stage contest: a written test to check knowledge in particular branches of law, and an essay to check the ability to present legal arguments, methods of interpretation and classification of case facts. In order to be admitted to the second stage of the contest the candidate must receive a minimum number of points, as set by the Minister of Justice. The written test and essay, together with regulations on the formulation are outlined by a contest team appointed by the Director of the National Polish School, under the advice of the Board. Tests, essay assignments and appropriate regulations are approved by the Minister of Justice.

Post-graduate legal trainees can be persons:

1. who are of Polish nationality and benefit from full civic and citizen rights;
2. who have unblemished reputation;
3. who have never been convicted with a legally binding sentence for an indictable offence or a fiscal offence;
4. against whom no criminal proceedings for an indictable offence or a fiscal offence are being conducted;
5. who have graduated from Master legal studies in the Republic of Poland or foreign legal studies recognised in the Republic of Poland;
6. who have been placed on the list.

A trainee is authorised to access the didactic and information base as well as the equipment and appliances in the Polish National School free of charge in order to further their knowledge and improve skills, on conditions defined by the Director of the Polish National School. Trainee's are obliged:

1. to attend classes, apprenticeship and internship schemes included in the curriculum;
2. to further their knowledge and practical skills individually, as described in the curriculum;
3. to take tests and examinations in terms stated in the curriculum;
4. to observe organizational regulations in the Polish National School and ordinances and directives of the Director of the Polish National School.

The Director of the National School awards a trainee with scholarship, on their request, for the term of the general post-graduate training and judge's training, with exemption of the period of internship.

The general post-graduate training last 12 months. The beginning of the general post-graduate training is fixed by the Minister of Justice by way of an ordinance published in the Public Information Bulletin. During the course of general training the trainees attend classes in the Polish National School and an apprenticeship scheme. The Director of the National School appoints to each trainee a mentor-coordinator to serve with substantial aid and to supervise and coordinate the proper course of apprenticeship. The Director of the National School together with the mentor-coordinator provides each trainee with a mentor for each apprenticeship scheme. The mentor introduces the trainee to activities falling under the scope of duties throughout the apprenticeship scheme. Immediately after the scheme has been completed, they will also submit to the mentor-coordinator a written assessment of the course of apprenticeship. The assessment reports and grades constitute the basis of the mentor-coordinator's final assessment review drafted together with a cumulative assessment of the course of all apprenticeship schemes attended by the trainee.

In order to complete the general post-graduate training, the participant has to gain positive grades on all tests and apprenticeship schemes attended as part of the training. A classification list of all trainees is published by the Director of the Polish National School in the Public Information Bulletin within 14 days after the post-graduate training is completed. The list includes full names and the total number of points gained by each trainee during the general training as well as the ordinal number pointing to their position on the list. At the end of the general post-graduate training, successful trainees receive a diploma issued by the Director of the Polish National School.

Judge's training

Each persons who has successfully completed the general training may apply to be placed on the classification list, also in the following training years, but no later than within 3 years after completed the general application. In this case, their position on the list is established according to the number of points gained during the general training they have completed. Candidates to the judge's post-graduate training are admitted by the Director of the Polish National School. Before accepting their duties, post-graduate legal trainees in the judge's or prosecutor's scheme swear to the Director of the Polish National School the following oath: "I solemnly swear to diligently perform duties of a trainee in the National School of the Judiciary and Prosecution Service, to act in accordance with rules of dignity and honesty, to care for the good name of the National School of the Judiciary and Prosecution Service and to keep all state, official and professional secrets", they may close the oath with a phrase: "So help me God".

The judge's post-graduate training lasts 54 months. Within the framework of training for judges, participants attend a 30-month-long course in the Polish National School and an apprenticeship scheme in accordance with the curriculum as well as serve a 24-month-long internship on the positions of assistant judge and a court referendary, in accordance with the curriculum. During the internship, the trainee judge is employed on the position of assistant judge under a contract of employment for a specified period of time, and subsequently on the position of court referendary for an unspecified period of time. Trainee judges take judiciary examination in the thirtieth month of training. In order to be entitled to take the judicial examination, the participant must gain positive notes on all tests and apprenticeship schemes attended as part of the training. The examination consists of a written and oral part. Practical tasks for the written paper and case studies for the oral paper of the judiciary examination are drafted by an examination team appointed by the Minister of Justice upon the request of the Director of the Polish National School commented by the Board.

Judges are appointed for an indefinite period by the President of the Republic on the motion of the National Council of the Judiciary. When appointing a judge, the President of the Republic of Poland indicates the place of service (the seat) of a judge. The change of the place of service of a judge may be made without the change of the post in cases and under special procedure.

Becoming a public notary

One of the most important legal professions in poland is public notary. It is practically impossible, under Polish law, to do any contract or service of any legal type without the presence of the public notary and his/her confirmation of the legality of the procedure. The profession is regulated in the Law on Public Notary of February 14, 1991[75] but is has existed in the Polish legal order since medival times. Notaries have their own bar association which is also responsible for the special apprenticeship program.

Entrance exam to the program constitutes of 150 multiple-choice questions and covers constitutional law, civil law and procedure, corporate and trade law, labor, family, administrative, financial as well as EU law.

Future notaries then fulfill a 2,5 year training including workshops, seminars as well as internships in courts and public notary offices. They observe all the procedures and study regulations necessary for the legal actions to be consistent with law. Final exam scheduled at the end of the apprenticeship program, if passed, guarantees the license to become a public notary. The apprenticeship is paid and known as the most difficult one to be completed.

75 Ustawa Prawo o notariacie, Dz. U. 2008, nr 189, poz. 1158.

Diplomatic and consular apprenticeship

Presented above five paths of professional education toward license to practice law are most popular among law graduates but not the only ones to be chosen. Depending on the scope of interest, future lawyer can work in different legal fields.

One possibility is to work in an international environment and pursue diplomacy goals. Under the auspicies of the Polish Ministry for Foreign Affairs, a special one-year training is offered to future diplomats and international officials called diplomatic and consular apprenticeship.

The entrance requirements include: certified knowledge of two foreign languages (as an alternative language tests may be taken at the Ministry) and passing of entrance exam – test covering major fields of constitutional, international and European law. The apprenticeship program is divided into two parts: theoretical (carried out by the Diplomatic Academy of the Polish Institute of International Affairs) and practical (internships at the organizational units of the Ministry for Foreign Affairs and foreign placements). The program ends with final diplomatic and consular exam. Graduates may further apply for positions on the diplomatic job market.

Marshal (sequestrator) apprenticeship

Becoming a marshal (debt collector) is one of the options for the law school graduates in Poland, as legal studies are required to participate in the further process of education. It is a very limited option. After the judge or advocate apprenticeship, you may work in a different legal profession, whereas here, once accepted, you can only work as marshal. As the job itself – collecting debts – is not the nicest work, it is then hardly surprising that for example in 2009, only 254 candidates from all over Poland took the entrance exam. The exam consists of 150 multiple -choice test questions. Based on the positive results, the Marhsal Chamber enrolls candidates who then begin their two-year apprenticeship program. Just like in other cases, the program includes theoretical elements (seminars, workshops, lectures, ect.) and practical elements (internships at the marshal offices). It is a paid education, as it is carried out by the National and local marshal chambers. The final step is the marshal exam scheduled at the end of the program. The final exam is didived into a written and oral part, both testing knowledge on procedural laws and court regulations.

Legislative apprenticeship

There is also a specific apprenticeship program designed to improve professional skills of the civil servants in field of legislative procedure. The employer may send a person involved in a legal job within the institution for two years to participate in this program and to become a legislator responsible for drafting of legal acts. The Government Center of Legislation organizes the training program. There are no scheduled entrance exams. Once nominated by the hiring institution, the candidate must go through an interview. There are an annually established number of available openings for this program. It lasts for 10 months and is based on some theoretical seminars, workshops and lectures as well as on practical tasks carried out under supervision of assigned practitioner. The final exam tests knowledge on legislative procedures in many legal systems, participants are requested to draft a particular act. There is also an oral part approving general knowledge of the future legislator. This apprenticeship program is expensive but the tuition is paid by the hiring institution as sort of investment in the employee.

Tax advisor

Becoming a tax advisor is also one of the options for law graduates with some professional experience. There is a requirement of at least 2 years of work in some legal profession (legal environment providing for legal experience) before a candidate can take a specially designed exam.

The exam is carried out by the Exam Commision for Tax Advise Affairs. There is a written part of the exam (100 multiple-choice questions) as well as draft of an oral statement representing a potential client in front of the court or tax organ. There is also an oral part of the exam – 10 questions to be answered after a 15 minutes preparation period. No training in a form of apprenticeship program is offered. Positive results of the exam constitute the only requirement for becoming a tax advisor in Poland.

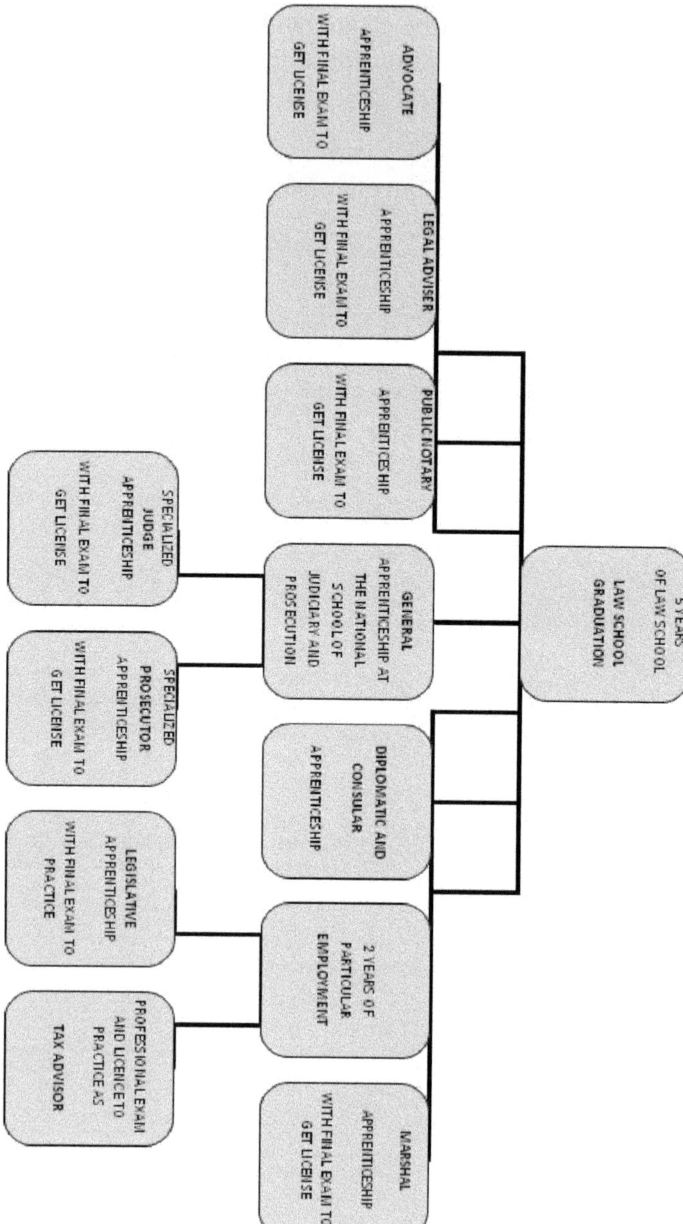
5 YEARS
OF LAW SCHOOL
LAW SCHOOL
GRADUATION
ADVOCATE
APPRENTICESHIP
WITH FINAL EXAM TO
GET LICENSE
LEGAL ADVISER
APPRENTICESHIP
WITH FINAL EXAM TO
GET LICENSE
PUBLIC NOTARY
APPRENTICESHIP
WITH FINAL EXAM TO
GET LICENSE
GENERAL
APPRENTICESHIP AT
THE NATIONAL
SCHOOL OF
JUDICIARY AND
PROSECUTION
SPECIALIZED
JUDGE
APPRENTICESHIP
WITH FINAL EXAM TO
GET LICENSE
SPECIALIZED
PROSECUTOR
APPRENTICESHIP
WITH FINAL EXAM TO
GET LICENSE
DIPLOMATIC AND
CONSULAR
APPRENTICESHIP
2 YEARS OF
PARTICULAR
EMPLOYMENT
LEGISLATIVE
APPRENTICESHIP
WITH FINAL EXAM TO
PRACTICE
PROFESSIONAL EXAM
AND LICENCE TO
PRACTICE AS
TAX ADVISOR
MARSHAL
APPRENTICESHIP
WITH FINAL EXAM TO
GET LICENSE

How to become a lawyer in Romania

Laura Magdalena TROCAN

Juridical education in Romania

In Romania, the essential condition for accessing the juridical professions is passing with a bachelor diploma the classes of a program of bachelor university studies of Law. The registration to such a program may be accomplished only after graduating high school (whose classes usually develop during 12 years) with a matriculation diploma and after passing an admission contest[76].

The programs of bachelor university studies in the Law field are organized both in the framework of the state universities and in the framework of the private universities[77]. For an university to establish

---

76 Considering that, in Romania, universities enjoy university autonomy (art. 123 of Law no. 1/2011 of national education), every university may establish the way they organize this admission contest, by respecting the general conditions imposed by the Ministry of Education, Research, Youth and Sports of Romania. In the recent years, some law faculties in Romania have chosen the option according to which the admission at the programs of Law bachelor university studies is accomplished by considering the general average obtained by candidates at the matriculation exam, and others have chosen for the admission to be accomplished based on the average obtained at an admission exam organized by them, consisting of supporting written tests in subjects studied in high school by the candidates, such as: Romanian language, History/Philosophy, Economy.

77 State universities in Romania in whose framework there are programs of Law bachelor university studies accredited or authorized to temporarily function: the University of Bucharest, "December 1st, 1918" University of Alba Iulia, Transilvania University of Braşov, Babeş-Bolyai University of Cluj Napoca, "Ovidius" University of Constanţa, the University of Craiova, "Dunărea de Jos" University of Galaţi, "Alexandru Iona Cuza" University of Iaşi, the University of Oradea, the University of Piteşti, "Lucian Blaga" University of Sibiu, "Ştefan cel Mare" University of Suceava, "Valahia" University of Târgovişte, "Constan-

such a study program, it should cross both a procedure of internal evaluation and a procedure of external evaluation, and the latter one is accomplished by the Romanian Agency of Providing Quality in Higher Education[78].

The considered evaluations are accomplished by respecting the Methodology of external evaluation, the standards and the list of the performance indicators of the Romanian Agency of Providing Quality in Higher Education[79]. According to the specific standards in the basic

---

tin Brâncuşi" University of Târgu-Jiu, "Petru Maior" University of Târgu-Mureş, Western University of Timişoara.
Private universities in Romania in whose framework there are programs of Law bachelor university studies accredited or authorized to temporarily function: "Dimitrie Cantemir" University of Bucureşti, "Titu Maiorescu" University of Bucureşti, "Nicolae Titulescu" University of Bucureşti, the Romanian-American University of Bucharest, Hyperion University of Bucharest, "Bioterra" University of Bucharest, the Ecological University of Bucharest, "Gheorghe Cristea" Romanian University of Sciences and Arts of Bucharest, "Vasile Goldiş" Western University of Arad, "George Bacovia" University of Bacău, "George Bariţiu" University of Braşov, "Bogdan Vodă" University of Cluj Napoca, "Andrei Şaguna" University of Constanţa, "Danubius" University of Galaţi, "Drăgan" European University of Lugoj, "Mihail Kogălniceanu" University of Iaşi, "Constantin Brâncoveanu" University of Piteşti, the Romanian-German University of Sibiu, "Tibiscus" University of Timişoara. (Decision of the Romanian Government no. 749/2009 for approving the List of the fields, of the structures of the higher educational structures and of the specializations/programs of bachelor university studies accredited or authorized to temporarily function, organized by them).

78 The Romanian Agency of Providing Quality in Higher Education is a full right member of the European Association for Providing Quality in Higher Education – ENQA. It is also registered in the European Registration for Providing Quality in Higher Education – EQAR <http://www.aracis.ro/>.

79 The Romanian Agency of Providing Quality in Higher Education is an autonomous public institution, of a national interest, with a juridical personality whose mission is to accomplish the external evaluation of the education quality provided by the higher education institutions and by other organizations supplying study programs specific to the higher education that operate in Romania in order to: test, based on the quality standards, the capacity of the organizations supplying education of satisfying the beneficiaries' expectations; contribute to the development of an institutional culture of the quality of the higher education and to

field of Juridical Sciences of the Romanian Agency of Providing Quality in the Higher Education – for the program of Law bachelor university studies, whether it is about frequency classes, classes with reduced frequency or at distance, the number of semesters is 8 (4 years), and the number of weeks for the years I, II, III is 14 per semester, and for the year IV, it is 12 (semester 7) and 10 (semester 8). Also, the total number of hours of organized activities, according to the educational plan, should be placed between 2200 – 2400. The specialty practice is optionally organized in the years I-III and compulsorily in semester 8 in courts and high courts, Prosecutor's Offices, lawyer offices and notarial offices, juridical consultancy companies, agencies, companies, town halls, institutions of the prefect, juridical directions in ministries etc.

In the educational plan of the programs of Law bachelor university studies, whether they are organized in the framework of state universities or of private ones, there should compulsorily appear the following:

I. Basic subjects: Constitutional Law and Public Institutions, General Theory of Law, Roman Law, Civil Law, Criminal Law;
II. Specialty subjects: Civil Procedural Law, Criminal Procedural Law, International Private Law, Commercial Law, International Trade Law, Work and Social Security Law, Administrative Law, International Public Law, Criminology, Intellectual Property Law, European Union Law, European Law of Competition, Environmental Law;
III. Complementary subjects: Financial Law, International Protection of Human Rights, Criminology/Juridical Sociology;
IV. Subjects of foreign languages and physical education.

---

provide the protection of the direct beneficiaries of study programs from the level of higher education by producing and disseminating systematic, coherent and credible, publically accessible information on the education quality, <http://www.aracis.ro/despre-aracis/misiune>.

Next to these subjects that should necessarily be found in the educational plan of the programs of Law bachelor university studies, each university may also introduce other juridical subjects or subjects of close scientific fields (for example, Organizing the Judicial System, Diplomatic and Consular Law, Mediating Conflicts, International Organizations and Relations, Civil Execution Law, International Humanitarian Law, International Criminal Law, Matrimonial Systems, Legal Medicine, Theory and Practice of Notarial Activity, Victimology, Juridical Protection of Human Rights, Compared Law, Bank and Exchange Law, Accounting Elements, Micro and Macroeconomy Elements, Transports Law, Juridical Logics, Protection of Personal Data, Law Philosophy, Political science, Rhetoric, History of Romanian Law, History of European Construction, Latin etc.).

Regarding the succession of the subjects in the educational plan, the standards of the Romanian Agency of Providing Quality in Higher Education show that:

I. In year I there will necessarily be General Theory of Law, Constitutional Law and Roman Law.
II. International Public Law will be studied after achieving the class of Constitutional Law and Public Institutions.
III. Financial Law will be studied after achieving the class of Administrative Law.
IV. Romanian Commercial Law will be taught after entirely achieving Civil Law.
V. Competition Law will be taught after achieving Commercial Law.
VI. International Trade Law will be taught after achieving Commercial Law and European Union Law.
VII. International Private Law will be studied after achieving Civil Law, Family Law, Civil Procedural Law.
VIII. Criminology, and also Legal Medicine, may be studied after achieving Criminal Law and Criminal Procedural Law.

The universities having in their structure faculties organizing programs of Law bachelor university studies should have informatics and criminology laboratories, and also judicial clinic laboratories[80]. Covering the subjects, especially the basic ones, should be accomplished by the official teachers in higher education based on a contest, having a PhD degree or postgraduates (in case of the dons developing seminary activities).

However, the didactic activities for the program of Law bachelor university studies may be also developed by practitioners having an experience of at least 5 years in a juridical field compatible with the profile of the subject where the didactic activity develops, and owning the scientific title of PhD, as associated teachers.

We should mention that, in Romania, the Bologna system was implemented starting with the university year 2005/2006, and according to Law no. 288/2004 regarding the organization of the university studies – regulating the organization of the university studies on three cycles, respectively bachelor university studies (corresponding to a number contained between minimum 180 and maximum 240 transferable study credits), master university studies (corresponding to a number contained between minimum 60 and maximum 120 transferable study credits) and PhD university studies (usually for 3 years) – in the juridical higher education in Romania, we also organize master university studies for 1-2 years and PhD studies by the institutions of higher education accomplishing the conditions established by the valid normative documents regarding the organization of such studies[81].

---

80 The specific standards in the basic field Juridical Sciences of the Romanian Agency of Providing Quality in the Higher Education, <http://www.aracis.ro/proceduri/>.

81 The Law Faculty of the University of Bucharest organizes the following master university studies: Judicial Career, Community Law, International Law, Advanced Private Law, Public Law, Business Law, Professional Master of European and International Law, Industrial and Work Relations, <http://www.unibuc.ro/facultati/drept/>.
The Law Faculty of Babeş-Bolyai University of Cluj-Napoca organizes the following master university studies: Criminal Sciences and Criminology, Private Law Institutions, Compared Private Law, European Law and National Business Law, Private Law of the European Union.

In the educational plan of the master university studies, there should be, depending on the master specific, subjects as: Public Law, Private Law, Criminal Sciences, Non-Contentious Administrative Procedure, Administrative Law and Administrative Contentious Law, Community Law and European Institutions, Financial and Bank Law, International Protection of Human Rights, Environmental Law, Environmental Community Law[82].

However, at present, the access to juridical professions, except for the magistrate profession (where the recruitment and the initial training of the magistrates is made only after graduating with a bachelor diploma a program of Law bachelor university studies and the courses of the National Institute of Magistracy of Bucharest, Romania), is not conditioned by graduating master or PhD university studies in the juridical field. For the programs of Law bachelor university studies organized in Romania, the studies end by supporting the bachelor exam that usually consists of two tests: a test of checking the accumulated knowledge in the basic and specialty subjects (usually, in Civil Law, Criminal Law, Civil Procedural Law and Criminal Procedural Law) and another test consisting of presenting the dissertation accomplished under the scientific coordination of a teacher, using a theme chosen by the student, in any of the subjects studied during the studying years, the latest at the beginning of the last university year. The ones passing this exam gain a bachelor diploma in Law.

<http://admitere.ubbcluj.ro/master-drept.html>.
The Law Faculty of "Alexandru Ioan Cuza" University of Iaşi organizes the following master university studies: Criminology, European Law, Criminal Sciences, Business Law, <http://laws.uaic.ro/admitere_master.html>.

82 The specific standards in the basic field *Juridical Sciences* of the Romanian Agency of Providing Quality in Higher Education, <http://www.aracis.ro/proceduri/>.

Access to juridical professions in Romania

The moment of ending the juridical studies represents a new beginning for every bachelor of Law[83]. Unlike the times before 1989, when the graduates of Law faculties were provided by the state with repartitions immediately after ending the studies, depending on the average grade, on the available jobs and on their options, at present, due to the political, economical and social changes interfered after December 1989, this system no longer works. Thus, the access both to the classic professions of law (magistrate, lawyer, notary, juridical counsellor, judicial executor etc.), and in the law professions existent in the public or private sector (for example, civil servant in the public administration, fiscal inspector, bank inspector, insurance inspector, custom agent, real estate agent, company administrator, mediator etc.) has known a series of new regulations that we will further try to synthesize.

How to become a magistrate (judge and prosecutor) in Romania

In Romania, the main normative documents regulating the organization and the exertion of the magistrate profession are: Law no. 304/2004 for the judicial organization, as further amended and completed; Law no. 303/2004 regarding the status of judges and prosecutors, as further amended and completed; Law no. 317/2004 regarding the Superior Council of Magistracy, as further amended and completed; Regulation of the National Institute of Magistracy approved by Decision no. 320/2005 of the Superior Council of Magistracy, as further amended and completed. According to art. 1 of Law no. 303/2004 regarding the status of judges and prosecutors, as further amended and completed "Magistracy is the judicial activity developed by judges in order to accomplish justice, and by prosecutors in order to protect the

83 C. Carp, D. Panainte, Guide of Law Student, C.H. Beck Press, Bucharest, 2006, p. 154.

general interests of society, of law order, and also of the citizens' rights and liberties".

We specify that, in Romania, the jobs of judge and prosecutor are incompatible with any other public or private jobs, except for the didactic jobs in the higher education, and also the training ones in the framework of the National Institute of Magistracy and of the National School of Actuaries, in the law conditions. The recruitment and the initial professional training of judges and prosecutors are made based on a contest, by the National Institute of Magistracy[84]. The date, the place, the way of developing the admission contest and the number of offered places[85] are made public by a release and they are published in the Official Gazette of Romania, Part III, on the website of the Superior Council of Magistracy and on the one of the National Institute of Magistracy, at least 60 days before the date established for the contest. According to art. 14, paragraph 1 of Law no. 303/2004 regarding the status of judges and prosecutors, as further amended and completed – the admission to the National Institute of Magistracy is made by respecting the principles of transparency and equality, exclusively based on a contest.

"The person who wants to register to the contest organized for the admission to the National Institute of Magistracy should cumulatively achieve the following conditions:

a) having a Romanian citizenship, a residence in Romania and a full capacity of exertion;
b) being a bachelor of Law;

---

84 The National Institute of Magistracy is a public institution with a juridical personality, situated in the coordination of the Superior Council of Magistracy of Romania, accomplishing the initial training of the future magistrates – judges and prosecutors –, the continuous professional training of the magistrates in function, and also the trainers' training, in the law conditions <http://www.inmlex.ro/index.php?MenuID=1>.

85 The Superior Council of Magistracy establishes every year the number of students, depending on the unoccupied jobs of judges and prosecutors, and also on the ones that will be established. (Art. 15, paragraph 4 of Law no. 303/2004 regarding the status of judges and prosecutors, as further amended and completed).

c) having no criminal records, no fiscal record and enjoying a good reputation;
d) speaking Romanian;
e) being medically and psychologically able to exert the function"[86].

The candidates declared as admitted to the National Institute of Magistracy are able to be justice listeners. They go to classes of professional training in the framework of the National Institute of Magistracy for 2 years. After the first class year, the justice listeners choose between the functions of judge and prosecutor, depending on the average and in report to the job numbers. During the classes, the justice listeners accomplish practice stages in the framework of the judicial courts and of the Prosecutor's Offices, assist to judicial meetings and the activity of criminal pursuit, in order to directly know the activities developed by the magistrates and by the specialty auxiliary staff. According to art. 17, paragraph 1 of Law no. 303/2004 regarding the status of judges and prosecutors, as further amended and completed – the justice listeners benefit from a scholarship having the feature of a monthly payment corresponding to the function of intern judge and prosecutor, in report to the seniority as they have as listeners.

At the same time, the lapse of time when a person has been a justice listener, if they promoted the graduation exam of the National Institute of Magistracy, constitutes the seniority for the job of judge or prosecutor[87]. After ending the classes at the National Institute of Magistracy, the justice listeners attend a graduation exam consisting of theoretical and practical tests by means of which they prove the appropriation of the knowledge necessary for exerting the function of judge or prosecutor. Justice listeners who passed the mentioned exam will be usually assigned, according to the law, in the functions which they chose after the first class year in the framework of the National Institute of Magistracy. The justice listeners who do not pass the grad-

---

86 Art. 14, paragraph 2 of Law no. 303/2004 regarding the status of judges and prosecutors, as further amended and completed.

87 Art. 17, paragraph 5 of Law no. 303/2004 regarding the status of judges and prosecutors, as further amended and completed.

uation exam may attend it once more at the next session organized by the National Institute of Magistracy. If the justice listener does not go to the exam, without a reason, or if he does not pass the exam in the second session, he cannot be assigned as a magistrate and he is forced to return the scholarship and the school expenditures. According to art. 20, paragraph 1 of Law no. 303/2004 regarding the status of judges and prosecutors, as further amended and completed – the bachelors of the National Institute of Magistracy are forced to accomplish the function of a judge or prosecutors for 6 years.

If a magistrate bachelor of the National Institute of Magistracy is released from his job before the expiration of the 6 year term, from his initiative or for reasons that are imputable to him, he is forced to return the justice listener scholarship and the school expenditures accomplished for his training, proportionally to the time remained until completing the 6 year term. The bachelors of the National Institute of Magistracy are intern judges and intern prosecutors for 1 year and they are assigned in function only in judicial courts or, where appropriate, at the Prosecutor's Offices near them, by the Superior Council of Magistracy, based on the results obtained at the graduation exam of the National Institute of Magistracy[88]. During the internship, the judges and the prosecutors are forced to continue the professional training, under the coordination of a judge or a prosecutor assigned by the president of the judicial court or, where appropriate, by the first prosecutor of the Prosecutor's Office near this court. After ending the internship, the intern magistrates are forced to attend the capacity exam. If the intern magistrate is rejected at the capacity exam, he is forced to attend the next session[89].

The unjustified absence from the capacity exam or the candidate's rejection in two sessions attracts the loss of the quality of intern judge or intern prosecutor, and in this case the intern magistrate should return the justice listener scholarship and the school expenditures. The

88 Art. 21 and art. 22 of Law no. 303/2004 regarding the status of judges and prosecutors, as further amended and completed.

89 Art. 25, paragraph 1 of Law no. 303/2004 regarding the status of judges and prosecutors, as further amended and completed.

candidates declared as admitted to the capacity exam have the right to choose their jobs, depending on their averages, in a 15 free day term since publishing them in the Official Gazette of Romania, Part III. In the circumscriptions of the courts and Prosecutor's Offices where a national minority has a weight of at least 50% of the inhabitants' number, at equal averages, the candidates speaking the language of that minority have priority[90].

The judges and prosecutors who promoted the capacity exam are assigned by Romania's President, at the suggestion of the Superior Council of Magistracy. At the same time, we should specify that they may assign in magistracy, based on a contest, if they accomplish the general conditions mentioned above required for the admission in magistracy, the former judges and prosecutors who stopped their activity for non-imputable reasons, the juridical specialty staff of the Ministry of Justice, the Public Ministry, the Superior Council of Magistracy, the National Institute of Criminology, the National Institute of Criminalist Expertises and the National Institute of Magistracy, the lawyers, the notaries, the judicial assistants, the juridical counsellors, the staff with probation with higher juridical studies, the officers of judicial police with higher juridical studies, the actuaries with higher juridical studies, the persons who accomplished juridical specialty functions in the device of Parliament, of Presidential Administration, of Government, of Constitutional Court, of People's Lawyer, of Account Court or of Legislative Council, of the Institute of Juridical Researches of the Romanian Academy and the Romanian Institute for Human Rights, the teachers in the accredited higher juridical education, and also the assistant-magistrates of the High Court of Cassation and Justice, with minimum a 5 year seniority in the specialty[91].

Exerting the magistrate profession in Romania imposes a series of interdictions and incompatibilities. Thus, according to art. 8 of Law

---

90 Art. 30, paragraph 6 of Law no. 303/2004 regarding the status of judges and prosecutors, as further amended and completed.

91 Art. 33 of Law no. 303/2004 regarding the status of judges and prosecutors, as further amended and completed.

no. 303/2004 regarding the status of judges and prosecutors, as further amended and completed – the judges and prosecutors are forbidden:

a) to develop commercial activities directly or by intermediary persons;
b) to develop arbitrage activities in civil, commercial or other kind of litigations;
c) to have the quality of associated or member of the organs of leadership, administration or control at the civil societies, commercial societies, including banks or other credit institutions, insurance societies or financial societies, national companies, national societies or autonomous overheads;
d) to be a member of a group of economical interest.

How to become a lawyer in Romania

In Romania, the main normative documents regulating the organization and exertion of the lawyer profession are: Law no. 51 of June 7th, 1995 for organizing and exerting the lawyer profession, as further amended, the Status of the lawyer profession published in the Official Gazette of Romania, Part I, no. 45/13.01.2005 and the Deontological Code of Lawyers in the European Union adopted of October 28th, 1998 and further amended in the Plenary Sessions of the Bar Council of the European Union (CCBE) of November 28th, 1998, December 6th, 2002 and May 19th, 2006[92].

In Romania, the lawyer profession is free and independent, with an autonomous organization and functioning, in the conditions of Law no. 51 of June 7th, 1995 for organizing and exerting the lawyer profession, as further amended, and of the profession status. The lawyer profession is exerted only by the lawyers registered in the table of the bar they belong to, a bar belonging to the National Union of Bars in Romania. The lawyer has the right to assist and represent the natural

92 This Code applies in Romania starting with January 1st, 2007, according to art. II of the Decision of the Permanent Commission of the National Union of Bars in Romania no. 1486/October 27th, 2007.

persons and the juridical entities in front of the courts of the judicial authority and of other jurisdiction organs, of the criminal pursuit organs, of the public institutions and authorities, and also in front of other natural persons or juridical entities that are forced to allow and provide to the lawyer the free development of his activity, in the law conditions[93]. According to art. 5 paragraph 1 of Law no. 51 of June 7th, 1995 for organizing and exerting the lawyer profession, as further amended:

"The types of exerting the lawyer profession are: individual parlours, associated parlours, professional civil societies or professional societies with a limited responsibility".

According to art. 12, paragraph 1 of Law no. 51 of June 7th, 1995 for organizing and exerting the lawyer profession, as further amended, a member of a bar of Romania should accomplish the following conditions:

a) he should exert civil and political rights;
b) he is a bachelor of a law faculty with the time established by the law;
c) he should not be found in any of the indignity cases stipulated by the current law;
d) he should be medically able to exert the profession[94].

In Romania the unworthy ones of being lawyers are:

a) the one permanently convicted by a judicial decision to prison for accomplished an intentional offence able to reach the profession prestige;
b) the one who accomplished abuses by means of which the basic human rights and liberties established by a judicial decision were disrespected or who accomplished serious disciplinary deviations

---

93 Art. 2, paragraph 3 of Law no. 51 of June 7th, 1995 for organizing and exerting the lawyer profession, as further amended.

94 The accomplishment of this conditions should be proved by a medical health certificate released based on the findings made by a medical commission constituted in the conditions stipulated in the profession status. (art. 12, paragraph 2 of Law no. 51 of June 7th, 1995 for organizing and exerting the lawyer profession, as further amended).

sanctioned by excluding him from the profession, as a disciplinary sanction;

c) the one who was forbidden to exert the profession on a term established by a juridical or disciplinary decision;

d) the fraudulent bankrupt, even if he was rehabilitated[95].

The member of a bar of another country may exert the lawyer profession in Romania, if he accomplishes the conditions of Law no. 51 of June 7th, 1995 for organizing and exerting the lawyer profession, as further amended[96].

At the same time, we should say that, in Romania, the exertion of the lawyer profession is incompatible with:

a) the waged activity in the framework of other professions different from the lawyer one;

b) the jobs injuring the dignity and independence of the lawyer profession or the good manners;

c) the direct exertion of material trade acts.

But, the exertion of the lawyer profession is compatible with:

a) the quality of deputy or senator, counsellor in the local or county councils;

b) didactic activities and functions in the higher juridical education;

c) the literary and publishing activity;

d) the quality of judge, mediator, conciliator or negotiator, fiscal counsellor, counsellor in intellectual property, counsellor in in-

---

95 Art. 14 of Law no. 51 of June 7th, 1995 for organizing and exerting the lawyer profession, as further amended.

96 For granting juridical consultancy regarding the Romanian law, the foreign lawyer is forced to attend an exam of checking the knowledge of Romanian law and Romanian language, organized by the National Union of the Bars in Romania. The foreign lawyer cannot put oral or written conclusions in front of the judicial courts and of the other jurisdictional and judicial organs, except for the ones of international arbitrage. The foreign lawyer exerting the profession in Romania is forced to register to the special table kept by every bar and it accepts the stipulations of the current law, of the profession status and of the deontological code. (Art. 13 of Law no. 51 of June 7th, 1995 for organizing and exerting the lawyer profession, as further amended).

dustrial property, authorized translator, administrator or liquidator in the framework of the procedures of reorganization and judicial liquidation, in the law conditions.

According to art. 17 of Law no. 51 of June 7th, 1995 for the organization and the exertion of the lawyer profession, as further amended – the receiving in the lawyer profession is accomplished only based on an exam organized by the National Union of the Bars in Romania, at national level, at least yearly. The exam for receiving in the lawyer profession is held at the National Institute for Preparing and Improving Lawyers and it is unitarily developed in its territorial centres, being based on a methodology elaborated and approved by the Council of the National Union of the Bars in Romania. The exam themes are unique at the level of the National Union of the Bars in Romania, and the subject selection is made by the national commission of exam[97].

Regarding the way of receiving in the profession, we should also say that, art. 17, paragraph 5 of Law no. 51 of June 7th, 1995 for organizing and exerting the lawyer profession, as further amended, stipulates that the judges of the High Court of Cassation and Justice of Romania, and also the Romanian judges of the international courts whose mandate expired or, who were released from the function for non-imputable reasons, may choose to go to the bar with no exam. The person passing the admission exam in the profession necessarily accomplishes a 2 year internship of professional training, under the guidance of a permanent lawyer with a seniority of at least 6 years in this quality and enjoying an intact professional reputation. During the

97 The national commission of exam is mainly formed of lawyers – dons having a seniority of minimum 10 years in the lawyer profession. Its assignment is made by the Permanent Commission of the National Union of the Bars in Romania, at the bars suggestion. (art. 17, paragraph 4 of Law no. 51 of June 7th, 1995 for organizing and exerting the lawyer profession, as further amended).

internship, the person passing the admission exam in the profession, will be an trainee lawyer[98].

The conditions of accomplishing the internship, the trainee lawyer's rights and obligations, the guiding lawyer's ones, and also the bar's ones to these are regulated by the profession status. The internship is suspended in case of a motivated absence from the profession or in case of stopping the professional guidance with no guilt of the trainee lawyer. According to art. 18, paragraph 3 of Law no. 51 of June 7th, 1995 for organizing and exerting the lawyer profession, as further amended, during the internship, with the agreement of the guiding lawyer, the trainee lawyer s may attend master classes that are considered when appreciating the initial professional training, in the conditions stipulated by the Status of the lawyer profession. After accomplishing the internship, the trainee lawyer will attend the finalisation exam. The trainee lawyer who was three times rejected at the finalisation exam will be excluded from the profession.

The quality of permanent lawyer[99] is gained based on an exam organized by the National Union of Bars in Romania, yearly and nationally, or by passing the graduation exam of the National Institute for Preparing and Improving Lawyers, in the conditions stipulated by the Status of the lawyer profession[100]. According to art. 20, paragraph 5,6,7 of Law no. 51 of June 7th, 1995 for organizing and exerting the lawyer profession, as further amended – the one who promoted the receiving exam in the lawyer profession and who accomplished the function of judge, prosecutor, notary public, juridical counsellor or lawyer for 5 years, until the date when attending the receiving exam in

98 The intern lawyer may put conclusions only at the judicial court. (art. 23, paragraph 1 of Law no. 51 of June 7th, 1995 for organizing and exerting the lawyer profession, as further amended).

99 The permanent lawyer has the right to put conclusions to all the courts, except for the High Court of Cassation and Justice and the Constitutional Court, where he could put conclusions if he has a continuous seniority in the profession of at least 5 years since the finalisation. (art. 23, paragraph 3 of Law no. 51 of June 7th, 1995 for organizing and exerting the lawyer profession, as further amended).

100 Art. 20, paragraph 1 of Law no. 51 of June 7th, 1995 for organizing and exerting the lawyer profession, as further amended.

the lawyer profession, gains the quality of a permanent lawyer, without attending the previously mentioned finalisation exam, only if he promotes the finalisation exam in the profession where he comes from.

The same stipulations apply to the persons who promoted the exam of entering the lawyer profession and who accomplished juridical specialty functions in the device of Parliament, of Presidential Administration, of Government, of Constitutional Court, of People's Lawyer, of Account Court and of Legislative Council, for 5 years without stopping. At the same time, the trainee lawyer who exerted at least one mandate of parliamentary, mayor, vice-mayor, president of the county council or vice-president of the county council, gains at the demand the quality of a permanent lawyer.

How to become a notary in Romania

In Romania, the main normative documents regulating the organization and the exertion of the notary profession are: Law no. 36 of May 12th, 1995 of notaries public and of the notarial activity, as further amended, the Regulation of applying the Law of notaries public and of the notarial activity no.36/1995, approved by the Order of the Ministry of Justice no.710/C/1995, as further amended, the Status of the National Union of Notaries public in Romania adopted by Congress VIII of Notaries public in Romania by Decision no. 12/21.11.2008 and the Deontological Code of Notaries public in Romania, adopted at the 3rd Congress of the National Union of Notaries public in Romania, 2001.

In Romania, the notary public accomplishes notarial acts such as: editing the documents with a juridical content, at the demand of the parties; the notarial succession procedure; certifying some acts, in the cases stipulated by the law; legalizing the signatures on documents, the specimens of signature, and also the seals; giving a certain date to the documents presented by the parties; receiving in the deposit the papers and the documents presented by the parties; legalizing the copies on the papers; accomplishing and legalizing translations[101]. At the same time, notaries public give juridical consultancies in notarial matter, different from the ones related to the content of the documents they accomplish and they participate, as specialists assigned by the parties, to the preparation and accomplishment of juridical notarial documents[102].

The public notaries' activity develops in the framework of an office where there may be one or several associated public notaries, with the corresponding auxiliary staff. In the circumscription of a judicial court, there may be one or several offices of public notaries. The number of notaries public and of the offices where they develop their activity is established by the minister of justice, at the suggestion of the Council of the National Union of Public Notaries.

According to art. 16 of Law no. 36 of May 12th, 1995 of notaries public and of the notarial activity, as further amended, in Romania, a notary public should accomplish the following conditions:

a) he should be a Romanian citizen and he should have a residence in Romania and he should have the ability of exerting civil rights;
b) he should be a bachelor of law – juridical sciences – or he should have a PhD in law;
c) he should have no criminal records;
d) he should enjoy a good reputation;
e) he should speak Romanian;
f) he should be medically able to exert the function;
g) he had accomplished the function of trainee notary for two years and he promoted the notary public exam[103] or he had exerted the

101 Art. 8 of Law no. 36 of May 12th, 1995 of public notaries and of the notarial activity, as further amended.

102 Art. 9 of Law no. 36 of May 12th, 1995 of public notaries and of the notarial activity, as further amended.

103 The public notary exam is held in front of a commission formed of: a member of the Council of the National Union of Notaries Public, the representative of the Ministry of Justice of Romania, a member of the didactic body of the higher specialty education and two notaries public enjoying a professional training and prestige, assigned in the conditions stipulated by the regulation of applying Law no. 36 of May 12th, 1995 of notaries public and of the notarial activity, as further

function of notary, judge, prosecutor, lawyer or another juridical specialty function for 5 years and he proves the knowledge necessary for the function of notary public, by passing an organized contest, according to the regulation of applying the current law, by the Council of the National Union of Notaries Public.

The notary public is assigned by the minister of justice, at the suggestion of the Council of the National Union of Notaries Public, based on the demand of the interested one and after proving the accomplishment of the requirements mentioned above. According to art. 36 of Law no. 36 of May 12th, 1995 of notaries public and of the notarial activity, as further amended, the exertion of the notary public profession is incompatible with:

a) the development of a waged activity or of a judicial executer, lawyer or juridical counsellor, except for:
   - the one of the university didactic activity;
   - the one of the literary and publishing activity;
   - the one of the quality of a deputy or a senator or of the quality of counsellor in the county or local councils, during the mandate;
   - the one of the membership to the leading organs or to other organisms of the National Union of Notaries Public, of the Chambers of Notaries Public or to other intern and international organizations where the National Union of Notaries Public and the Chambers of Notaries Public are affiliated or which they collaborate with;
b) the development of commercial activities, directly or by means of intermediary persons;
c) the quality of an associate in a society in a collective name, of a sole shareholder in simple or share partnerships or on actions, of an administration of a limited liability company, of a president of an administration council, of a member of a leading council, of a

---

amended. (Art. 22 of Law no. 36 of May 12th, 1995 of notaries public and of the notarial activity, as further amended).

general executive or of an executive of a share company, of an administrator of a civil company.

How to become a judicial executor in Romania

In Romania, the main normative documents regulating the organization and exertion of the judicial executor profession are: Law no. 188/2000 referring to judicial executors, as further amended, Regulation of applying Law no. 188/2000 regarding the judicial executors, the Status of the National Union of Judicial Executors and of the judicial executor profession of September 3rd, 2010, published in the Official Gazette of Romania, Part I no. 713 of October 26th, 2010.

In Romania, the forced execution of the civil stipulations of the executory titles are accomplished by the judicial executors, except for the situations when the law stipulates differently. According to art. 12, paragraph 1 of Law no. 188/2000 related to the judicial executors, as further amended, the activity of the judicial executors develops in an office where there may be one or several associated judicial executors, with the corresponding auxiliary staff. According to art. 14 of Law no. 188/2000 referring to judicial executors, as further amended - in the circumscription of a judicial court there may be one or several judicial executors whose competence lies on the whole content of the appeal court in whose territorial area the judicial court is placed.

In Romania, a judicial executor should accomplish the following conditions stipulated by art. 15, letters a-g of Law no. 188/2000 referring to judicial executors, as further amended:

a) he should be a Romanian citizen and he should have a residence in Romania;
b) he should have a full exertion capacity;
c) he should be a bachelor of law;
d) he should have no criminal records and he should enjoy a good reputation;
e) he should speak Romanian;
f) he should be medically able to exert the function;

g) he had accomplished the function of an intern judicial executor for 2 years[104] and he promoted the finalisation exam or, where appropriate, he had exerted a juridical specialty function for 3 years and he promoted the admission contest or exam in the profession.

The persons dispensed from the exam are the ones who had exerted the function of a judge, a prosecutor or a lawyer for 5 years, only if they promoted the finalisation exam in the profession where they come from[105]. The judicial executor is assigned by the minister of justice, in the circumscription of a judicial court, based on the demand of the interested one and after checking the accomplishment of the conditions mentioned above. According to art. 44, paragraph 1 of Law no. 188/2000 referring to judicial executors, as further amended - the judicial executors are forced to participate at least once in 3 years to program s of continuous professional training organized by the National Union of Judicial Executors , by the chambers of judicial executors near the appeal courts, by the higher educational institutions in the country or abroad or by other types of professional improvement. We should say that, in Romania, the exertion of the judicial executor function is incompatible with:

---

104 A judicial executor should accomplish the conditions stipulated by art. 15, letters a-f of Law no. 188/2000 referring to judicial executers, as further amended , he promoted the admission contest or exam in the judicial executor profession, organized by the National Union of Judicial Executers, under the coordination and control of the Ministry of Justice, he was in internship until promoting the capacity exam and he is employed in a judicial executor office.
The admission contest or exam in the judicial executor profession is organized yearly or anytime it is necessary, by the National Union of Judicial Executers, under the coordination and the control of the Ministry of Justice. The date and the place of developing the contest or the exam are established by an order of the minister of Justice, by consulting the National Union of Judicial Executers. The admission contest or exam in the judicial executor profession and the finalisation exam will develop in front of a commission containing necessarily representatives of the National Union of Judicial Executers, of the Ministry of Justice and dons of the higher specialty education.

105 Art. 15 of Law no. 188/2000 referring to judicial executers, as further amended.

a) the waged activity in the framework of other professions, except for the university didactic activity, the artistic, literary and publishing activity;
b) the quality of a deputy or a senator or a counsellor in the county or local councils, during the mandate;
c) the development of commercial activities, directly or by intermediary persons;
d) the quality of an associate to a company in a collective name, a silent associate in simple partnerships or in share company, an administrator of a limited liability company, a president of an administration council, a member of the leading council, a general executive or an executive of a society on actions, and administrator of a professional company[106].

How to become a juridical counsellor in Romania

In Romania, the main normative documents regulating the organization and the exertion of the juridical counsellor profession are: Law no. 514 of November 28th, 2003 regarding the organization and the exertion of the juridical counsellor profession, Law 246/2006 for completing Law no. 514/2003 regarding the organization and the exertion of the juridical counsellor profession, the Status of the juridical counsellor profession adopted by the Extraordinary Congress of the Colleges of Juridical Counsellors in Romania of March 6th, 2004 and published in the Official Gazette of Romania, Part I, no. 684 of July 29th, 2004. According to the stipulations of art. 1 of Law no. 514 of November 28th, 2003 regarding the organization and the exertion of the juridical counsellor profession – the al counsellor provides the protection of the legal rights and interests of the state, of the central and local public authorities, of public and public interest institutions, of the other juridical entities of private law, in whose service he is and according to Romania's Constitution and laws.

---

106 Art. 42 of Law no. 188/2000 referring to judicial executers, as further amended.

In Romania, the juridical counsellor may be assigned in function or employed in work, in law conditions. According to art. 3 of Law no. 514 of November 28th, 2003 regarding the organization and the exertion of the juridical counsellor profession – the juridical counsellor assigned in function has the status of the functionary, according to its functions and category, and the juridical counsellor employed in work has the status of a wage-earner. The juridical counsellor, in his activity, provides consultancy and the representation of the public authority or institution in whose service he was or of the juridical entity he has work reports with, he protects their legal rights and interests in their reports with the public authorities, the institutions of any kind, and also with any juridical entity or natural person, either Romanian or foreign; in law conditions and in the ones of the regulations specific to the unit, he advises and countersigns juridical documents[107].

In Romania, a juridical counsellor should accomplish the following conditions:

a) he should be a Romanian citizen and he should have a residence in Romania;
b) he should have the exertion of civil and political rights;
c) he should be a bachelor of a law faculty;
d) he should be medically able to exert the profession;
e) he should be in no situation such as the indignity cases stipulated by the current law[108].

The citizen of a member state of the European Union or of the European Economical Space may exert the juridical counsellor profession in Romania, if he accomplishes the conditions mentioned above, except for the one related to the Romanian citizenship. Such a person who gained the qualification of a juridical counsellor in the original member state may require anytime the acknowledgement of the di-

107 Art. 4 of Law no. 514 of November 28th, 2003 regarding the organization and the exertion of the juridical counsellor profession.

108 Art. 8 of Law no. 514 of November 28th, 2003 regarding the organization and the exertion of the juridical counsellor profession.

plomas, in order to be admitted as a juridical counsellor of practicing it in Romania[109].

In order to acknowledge the diplomas in Romania, the applicant will have to attend, of his choice, an exam of checking the knowledge or to accomplish a 3 year internship in the Romanian law field. One cannot be a juridical counsellor if:

a) they were permanently sentenced for accomplishing an offence such as injuring the juridical counsellor profession;
b) in exerting the juridical counsellor profession, they accomplished abuses by means of which they disrespected the basic human rights and liberties established by an irrevocable judicial decision;
c) they were declared as unworthy for other causes by the law[110].

According to art. 10 of Law no. 514 of November 28th, 2003 regarding the organization and the exertion of the juridical counsellor profession – exerting the juridical counsellor profession is incompatible with:

a) being a lawyer;
b) the activities injuring the dignity and independence of the juridical counsellor profession or the good manners;
c) any other authorized or waged profession in the country or abroad;
d) the function and the activity of an administrator or a liquidator in the framework of the procedures of reorganization and judicial liquidation;
e) the waged publishing activity;
f) other incompatibilities stipulated by the law or resulting from an interest conflict, in law conditions.

The exertion of the juridical counsellor profession is compatible with:

a) the university didactic activity and the juridical research one, the non-waged literary, cultural and publishing activity;

---

109 Art. 8 of Law no. 514 of November 28th, 2003 regarding the organization and the exertion of the juridical counsellor profession.

110 Art. 9 of Law no. 514 of November 28th, 2003 regarding the organization and the exertion of the juridical counsellor profession.

b) the function of an arbiter, a mediator or an expert, in law conditions and by respecting the legal stipulations regarding the interest conflicts;
c) participating to study commissions of accomplishing projects of juridical regulations[111].

According to art. 12, paragraph 1 of Law no. 514 of November 28th, 2003 regarding the organization and the exertion of the juridical counsellor profession – at the beginning of exerting the profession, the juridical counsellor necessarily accomplishes a 2 year internship of professional training, a lapse of time when he is an intern juridical counsellor. Art. 13, paragraph 1 and 2 stipulates the following: the intern juridical counsellor puts conclusions at the judicial court and at courts such as the basic court, at the criminal pursuit organs, and also at the other administrative organs having jurisdictional attributions, and the permanent juridical counsellor may put conclusions at the judicial courts of any degree, at the criminal pursuit organs, and also at all the authorities and administrative organs having jurisdictional attributions. The activity of a juridical counsellor is considered as seniority in the juridical work in the functions of magistrate, lawyer, notary public or other juridical functions, according to the legal stipulations specific to each of these professions[112].

How to become an actuary/registrar in Romania

In accomplishing the justice act, the actuaries/registrar' work constitutes a real support for the magistrates, and the competence and the correct accomplishment of the tasks belonging to them are important for the good development of the entire activity of the judicial courts. At present, in Romania, the actuary profession is regulated by Law

111 Art. 11 of Law no. 514 of November 28th, 2003 regarding the organization and the exertion of the juridical counsellor profession.
112 Art. 7 of Law no. 514 of November 28th, 2003 regarding the organization and the exertion of the juridical counsellor profession.

no.567/2004 regarding the status of the auxiliary staff in the courts and Prosecutor's Offices, as further amended and Law no.304/2004 regarding the judicial organization, as further amended, whose stipulations were detailed by the functioning regulations of the judicial courts and of the Prosecutor's Offices near them.

According to the stipulations of Law no. 567/2004, as further amended, the specialty auxiliary staff of the judicial courts and of the Prosecutor's Offices near them is formed of: actuaries (for meetings); statistician actuaries/registrars; documentarian actuaries/registrars; archivist actuaries/registrars; registering actuaries/registrars; IT specialists[113].

The actuary recruitment is usually made by the National School of Actuaries/Registrars but, whereas the National School of Actuaries/ Registrars in Romania has no capacity necessary for training enough new actuaries, the law also allows the organization of contests of direct occupation of the actuary jobs, contests organized by the appeal courts or by the Prosecutor's Offices near them, or by the High Court of Cassation and Justice of Romania or by the Prosecutor's Office near it, if, due to the big number of unoccupied jobs, the activity development is seriously affected. An actuary/registrar should accomplish the following conditions: he should be a Romanian citizen and he should have a residence in Romania and he should have the full exertion capacity; he should have no criminal records, no fiscal records and he should enjoy a good reputation; he should speak Romanian; he should be medically able to exert the function; he should have higher specialty studies (for accomplishing this condition, it is necessary to graduate higher juridical studies) or average studies[114], com-

113 <http://www.grefieri.ro/default.asp?nod=14>.

114 For assigning a statistician actuary, they need to be bachelors of higher economical studies, higher juridical studies or average economical studies. For assigning a documentarian actuary, they need to be bachelors of higher juridical studies, higher studies of public administration or of philology or average studies.

puter skills or typing skills; he should be a bachelor of the National School of Actuaries/Registrars [115].

Access to law professions existing in the public or private sector (for example, a civil servant in the local and central public administration, a fiscal inspector, a bank inspector, an insurance inspector, a custom agent, a real estate agent, a company administrator, a mediator etc.)

In Romania, the access to such professions is usually accomplished by a contest announced at least 30 days before organizing it, consisting of attending written and/or oral tests based on themes specific to every field and priorly announced, but one of the registration conditions to such a contest is to be a bachelor of a law faculty or of another faculty that could offer the skills necessary for correspondingly accomplishing the attributions involved by that job.

The requirement of the juridical studies is necessary, considering the fact that the development of the current activities of the firms and companies of the public and private field imposes the existence of specialists owning knowledge of financial law, commercial law, work law, insurance law, international private law, international trade law, bank and exchange law, fiscal law, the legislation of constructions and territory arrangement etc.

In the framework of public administration, the bachelors of law may have different functions such as: secretaries of local councils, civil servants in different departments of the local and central public administration etc. Graduating the juridical studies also offer the possibility to build a career in the field of diplomacy and international relations.

Thus, according to the stipulations of Law no. 269/2003 regarding the Status of the Diplomatic and Consular Body of Romania, the membership to the Diplomatic and Consular Body of Romania may be

115 Art. 33 of Law 567/2004 regarding the status of the specialty auxiliary staff of the judicial courts and of the Prosecutor's Offices near them.

gained by the person who accomplishes cumulatively the following conditions:

a) he has the right to occupy a public function, according to the stipulations of the valid Constitution and laws;
b) he enjoys all the political and civil rights stipulated in the valid Constitution and laws;
c) he is not part of political parties;
d) he attended long-term higher studies at a higher educational institution in the country or abroad, graduated with a bachelor diploma or with an equivalent one, acknowledged by the Ministry of Education and Research;
e) he speaks at least one foreign language;
f) he has a correspondingly health state attested based on a special medical document emitted by the medical centre working for the Ministry of Extern Affairs;
g) he graduated the Diplomatic Academy or he promoted the admission contest in the Diplomatic and Consular Body of Romania, organized according to the regulation of organization and development of the admission contest in the Ministry of Extern Affairs;
h) he has not been sentenced for accomplishing any offence.

Another profession where the bachelors of the law faculties in Romania is the mediator one. According to art. 7 of Law 192/2006 regarding the mediation and the organization of the mediator profession, as further amended, a mediator should accomplish the following conditions:

a) he should have a full exertion capacity;
b) he should have higher studies;
c) he should have a minimum 3 year work seniority;
d) he should be medically able to exert this activity;
e) he should enjoy a good reputation and he should not have been permanently sentenced for accomplishing an intentional offence able to injure the profession prestige;
f) he should have graduated the classes for training mediators, in law conditions, or a post-university program such as a master in

the field, accredited according to the law and advised by the Mediation Council;

g) he should have been authorized as a mediator, in the conditions of the current law.

The persons accomplishing these conditions will be authorized as mediators by the Mediation Council. The citizens of the member states of the European Union, of the European Economical Space or of the Swiss Confederation, owners of a qualification document in the mediator profession obtained in one of these states, gain, in the context of the establishment law, the access to the profession in Romania, after the Mediation Council acknowledges these documents.

Conclusions

The examination of the aspects regarding the organization and the exertion of these professions proves that a diploma in the law field creates the premises necessary for accessing numerous juridical professions, offering a larger scale of using the knowledge and the competences. These aspects were also the ones that have determined, in the last 20 years, based on the changes interfered in the Romanian society, the increase of the number of public or private universities offering program s of bachelor university studies in this field.

At the same time, we should mention that obtaining a university diploma in the law field opens the way for an important juridical career, but it imposes a deepening of the theoretical studies and a continuous practical training, considering the legislation evolution.

How to become a lawyer in Portugal and in Spain

Guilherme Waldemar D'OLIVEIRA MARTINS & Raquel FRANCO

Portugal

In Portugal lawyers are independent professionals holding a law degree who represent their clients at law and provide for legal advice on a professional and paid basis.

Only lawyers and probationary lawyers registered with the respective Portuguese Bar Association may practice professionally and, in particular, represent their clients at law or provide for legal advice as paid independent professionals.

The abovementioned does not apply to legal agents *(Solicitadores)* registered with their own professional association *(Câmara dos Solicitadores)* and who have their own particular status. Also, it should be noted that the provision of legal advice by persons holding a law degree who are public officials or who operate in an employed capacity does not require registration in the Portuguese Bar Association in cases where the advice is given to the individual's employer. On the other hand, the teaching staff in faculties of law who merely provide for written legal opinions are not legally deemed to be practicing lawyers and are not, therefore, required to be registered with that Association.

Prerequisites

Becoming a lawyer in Portugal involves meeting a set of prerequisites, educational requirements and professional duties.

The prerequisites relate primarily to the fact that lawyers are considered to play a part in the administration of justice, with the exclusive competence – subject to the exceptions laid down in law – to represent the parties with full technical discretion and bound solely by constraints of legality and the rules of professional ethics.

Therefore, as servants of justice and the law, lawyers are required – as a prerequisite to joining the Bar as well as throughout their careers – to prove themselves worthy of the honor and responsibilities inherent in that role. For instance, when exercising their profession, lawyers are required to maintain absolute independence and objectivity at all times and must not use their role to pursue any goals other than professional ones, complying fully with the duties set out in law and those arising from custom, practice and tradition.

The prerequisites demanded from someone who wants to become a lawyer include having the moral integrity to exercise the profession, being in full possession of civil rights, not having been declared incapable of administering themselves and their goods by final judgment, not being incompatible or disqualified for the practice of law. Furthermore, if the candidate was previously a magistrate, employee or agent, he or she can not have been dismissed, retired or placed on inactivity due to lack of moral character through a disciplinary process.

As for the educational requirements, it is only necessary to have a law degree, whether obtained in Portugal or in another EU country or country with which Portugal has entered into an agreement granting the necessary equivalence.

A person who possesses a recognized law degree and meets all of the aforementioned prerequisites can become a lawyer in Portugal by joining the Portuguese Bar Association. Being a member of a professional law association ensures that those engaged in the profession practice it correctly, both in the public interest and in that of the members.

Traineeship period

In order to do that, the candidate should apply to the Portuguese Bar Association and complete a traineeship period (*Estágio*), although it can be waived in the case of Professors and former Professors from Faculties of Law and holders of a doctorate in Law. The traineeship period includes both theoretical and practical components as well as two periods of examination in which the candidates are either approved or excluded from the rest of the traineeship.

If approved, the candidate, who up until which was a trainee lawyer (Advogado Estagiário) shall become a full lawyer (Advogado). Membership to the Portuguese Bar Association implies paying for the respective fees and agreeing to abide by the Association's ethics guidelines. Also, the lawyer should register with the tax authorities, contract insurance with a company that provides insurance policies for practicing lawyers in Portugal and sign up with the Caixa de Previdência dos Advogados e Solicitadores (an independent social security body for lawyers and solicitors only). These obligations are also extended to trainee lawyers.

Foreign citizens

Moreover, according to Article 14 of Regulation 232/2007 (Regulation of Inscription of Lawyers and Trainee Lawyers), foreign citizens who have obtained their degree in Portugal may be registered in the Portuguese Bar Association in the same way as Portuguese citizens if their country of nationality grants identical rights to Portuguese citizens. For that purpose the foreign citizens who wish to register with the Portuguese Bar Association must submit an application to the district council of the Bar.

On the other hand, according to Article 17 of Regulation 232/2007, Brazilian citizens with a degree from any Faculty of Law in Portugal or Brazil which are legally qualified to practice law in Brazil, may register with the Portuguese Bar Association insofar a reciprocity regime applies to Portuguese lawyers registered in the Portuguese Bar Association who wish to register in the Brazilian Law Association. Additionally, persons authorized for professional activity in their respective European Union Member State under one of the following professional titles are recognized as lawyers in Portugal and are therefore permitted to work in the profession:

- In Belgium: Avocat/Advocaat/Rechtsanwalt;

- In Denmark: Advokat;
- In Germany: Rechtsanwalt;
- In Greece: δικηγόρος;
- In Spain: Abogado/Advocat/Avogado/Abokatu;
- In France: Avocat; In Ireland: Barrister/Solicitor;
- In Italy: Avvocato;
- In Luxembourg: Avocat;
- In the Netherlands: Advocaat;
- In Austria: Rechtsanwalt;
- In Finland: Asianajaja/Advokat;
- In Sweden: Advokat;
- In the United Kingdom: Advocate/Barrister/Solicitor.

Any of these professionals may operate in Portugal under their original professional title expressed in the official language concerned and with an indication of the professional organization with which they are registered or of the jurisdiction within which they are entitled to practice under the law of their State of origin. However, legal representation or mandates in the Portuguese courts may only be undertaken by lawyers from the European Union operating with their original professional designation and under the guidance of a lawyer who is a member of the Portuguese Bar Association.

Nevertheless, lawyers from the European Union may, subject to prior registration with the Portuguese Bar Association, operate in Portugal under the designation of Advogado.

Occasional provision of professional services

Another way of practicing law in Portugal is through the occasional provision of professional services by lawyers from the European Union practicing under their original professional designation. This is allowed, but prior notice must be given to the Portuguese Bar Association.The installation in Portuguese territory of a permanent establishment by lawyers from the European Union wishing to practice under the professional title of their place of origin also requires prior registration with the Portuguese Bar Association. Registration entails the presentation of a practicing certificate from the Member State of

origin and of an additional certificate making evidence that this right has not been suspended or withdrawn as a result of criminal or disciplinary proceedings. These documents may also be demanded from lawyers supplying advocacy services in the manner mentioned above.
Incompatibilities

The lawyer profession is incompatible with any activity or role which diminishes the independence and dignity of the profession. Here, the Articles of Association of the Portuguese Bar Association set out a wide range of activities considered to be incompatible with the practice of the profession of lawyer.

Law firms

Lawyers can exercise their activity individually or through a law firm. According to Decree Law 229/2004, that establishes the legal regime of law firms, only lawyers can participate in law firms, irrespective of registration in Portugal or in any other Member State of the European Union. According to the same legislation, the draft articles of association of a law firm are required to be subject to prior approval by the General Council of the Portuguese Bar Association. This body exercises a strict legality control, namely by checking whether the articles of association are in accordance with the ethical standards set out in the Statute of the Bar, as well as with other laws deemed applicable.
Fees

A final note is due on the subject of lawyers' fees. These are charged for the services provided and can be paid in the form of a fixed fee, periodic payments or fees per hour. However, contingent fees, i.e. agreements entered into by lawyers and their clients prior to the conclusion of a proceeding whereby the client undertakes to pay the lawyer only a percentage of the benefit obtained when the proceeding concludes are forbidden regardless of being a sum of money or some other kind of benefit, asset or value, except if the agreement also includes a lump sum payment.

Spain

Becoming a lawyer in Spain is a rather straightforward process which depends upon meeting a set of prerequisites, educational requirements and professional duties.

Prerequisites

The prerequisites are three: the first is being a Spanish national or a national of another EU Member State or of a country that is a party to the 1992 Agreement creating the European Economic Area; the second is to be of age, which means having at least 18 years old and not being mentally incapacitated. The third one is not being disqualified for any reason from practicing as a lawyer, which implies not having a prior criminal record and not being in a situation of incompatibility with the exercise of the profession.

As for the educational requirements, it is capital to have a law degree, whether obtained in Spain or in another country that is part of the European Union or with which Spain has entered into an agreement. Under the Lawyers' Statute, lawyers from other countries may provide professional services in Spain in accordance with the applicable legislation, which distinguishes between two different groups:

- Nationals of EU Member States and, under the Agreement creating the European Economic Area signed in Oporto on 2 May 1992 and ratified by Spain on 26 November 1993, nationals of the EEA States. In accordance with the principle of free circulation of persons and services in the Member States, there are at present various different alternatives:
  - The right to practice for an indefinite period with the qualification obtained in the country of origin, with the possibility of incorporation into the profession after three years' effective and regular practice.
  - Recognition of the professional qualification obtained in the country of origin, recognizing the right to practice on the same terms as holders of the Spanish qualification.
  - Occasional provision of professional services using the qualification obtained in the country of origin.

  - In addition, persons not qualified to practice in their country of origin but holding the foreign qualification required for access to the profession may apply for recognition of this qualification in Spain and subsequently register with the Spanish Bar Association.
- Persons who are not nationals of an EU or EEA Member State:
  - In order to become a member of a Spanish Bar Association, these persons must first have their qualifications officially recognized and then apply for a *dispensa legal de nacionalidad* (exemption on the grounds of nationality).

On the other hand, one who already holds a law degree from another country should check with his or her University or with the Spanish ministry of education whether his or her degree is automatically recognized by the European Union or by any other international agreement as an equivalent degree. If so, the educational requirements needed in order to becoming a lawyer in Spain are fulfilled. If the law degree obtained in a foreign university is not automatically recognized through international agreements as a Spanish equivalent, it is also possible to apply with the Spanish ministry of education in order to obtain the evaluation of the degree and subsequent recognition as equivalent to a law degree earned in Spain. If the application is approved and the law degree is duly recognized as a Spanish equivalent, the educational requirements for becoming a lawyer in Spain will then be fulfilled.

Appliance

A person being in possession of a recognized law degree and meeting all of the three prerequisites mentioned above can become a lawyer in Spain by joining the Spanish Bar Association (Colegio de Abogados). In order to do that, the candidate should find a local Bar Association, preferably according to the place in which he or she will work and/or live and apply. There is a full list of all the Colegios de Abogados across Spain on the Consejo General de la Abogacia Espanola website. That does not involve, however, restricting the practice of law in that area since lawyers in Spain may freely practice law throughout the country and also in the European Union or in other countries as may be provided for by law. Signing up with the Bar Association implies paying for the applicable fees, and agreeing to abide by the association's ethics guidelines. Also, the lawyer should contract insurance with a company that provides insurance policies for practicing lawyers in Spain and sign up with Spanish social security at the social security office.

Lawyers are independent members of a liberal profession who provide a service to society. They are not civil servants and practice on the basis of free and fair competition (Article 1 of the Lawyers' Statute).

Lawyers must comply with laws and statues and with the code of ethics and conduct for the profession. The following bodies are responsible for ensuring that lawyers exercise their functions correctly:

– at national level, the General Council of Lawyers;
– in each Autonomous Community, the Council of the Bar Associations in that Community;
– in each province, the provincial or district Bar Associations.

Under Article 436 of the Organic Law on the Judiciary and Article 8 of the Lawyers' Statute, lawyers (*abogados*) perform the following functions:

– Advising and defending: parties to all kinds of legal proceedings (civil, criminal, administrative, employment and military); vis-à-vis administrative bodies, associations, corporations and public agencies of any kind; vis-à-vis any private entity or individual where necessary in the exercise of their functions.
– Legal advice and counseling.
– Representation of the client except when such practice is reserved by law to other professions.

In accordance with the referred legislation, legal professionals in Spain are engaged in two main areas: the prevention and settlement of disputes.

On the one hand, the main professions in the area of prevention of disputes are those that ensure legal certainty through advice, documentation or registration services. On the other hand, the main professions engaged in the settlement of disputes are those involved in litigation. Some of these (usually the liberal professions) direct and represent the parties, while others, members of the judiciary who form part of the public administration, direct legal proceedings and decide on disputes.

In the area of prevention of disputes the main professions are lawyers (*abogados*), who provide for legal advice, notaries, who provide for documentation, attestation and advisory services, property and commercial registrars, who keep public registers recording important legal acts that may affect third parties, check that documents entered in the register conform to legal requirements and advise persons who wish to make entries in the register.

In the area of settlement of disputes the main professions are lawyers, who direct the parties to litigation and settle disputes through the alternative systems in place, court lawyers (*procuradores*), who represent the parties in court, court clerks (*secretarios judiciales*), who are responsible for documentation and for expediting legal proceedings and judges (*jueces* and *magistrados* – *magistrados* are judges sitting in higher courts), who rule on disputes.

In addition to the professions listed above, there are other professionals who deal with legislative matters and who are therefore required to hold a special qualification (not necessarily a law degree) in a particular area of law and be a member of a professional association.

This category includes the holders of certain diplomas, e.g. "*graduados sociales*" (consultants on labor and social security matters who handle these matters for companies, individuals, etc.). Holders of these qualifications who belong to the relevant professional associations may represent the parties in labor law proceedings.

Also, a special category of lawyers should be named: court lawyers (procuradores) represent the rights and interests of the parties in the law courts through a power of attorney granted for this purpose, and ensure that communications between the courts and the parties are duly authenticated.

In order to qualify as a court lawyer it is necessary to have Spanish nationality, to be of age, to hold a law degree and to have obtained the title of procurador, which is granted by the Ministry of Justice to applicants who have fulfilled the requirements.

In order to practice as a procurador it is necessary to register with a Colegio de Procuradores, deposit a bond and swear an oath or promise to the court.

Law firms

In Spain lawyers can exercise their activity individually or through a law firm. According to the legal regime of law firms these can be multidisciplinary (*régimen de colaboración multiprofesional*) as long as the common exercise of the two or more activities is not incompatible in face of the applicable legislation.

Fees

Finally, in what concerns the payment of lawyer's services, similarly to what was described as being the regime applicable in Portugal, lawyers' fees are charged for the services provided and can be paid in the form of a fixed fee, periodic payments or fees per hour. Contingent fees are forbidden, i.e. agreements entered into by lawyers and their clients prior to the conclusion of a proceeding whereby the client undertakes to pay the lawyer only a percentage of the benefit obtained for the client when the proceeding concludes, regardless of whether this is a sum of money or some other kind of benefit, asset or value.
The amount of the fee can be fixed freely by the client and the lawyer provided it does not infringe the professional code of ethics or the rules of fair competition. If the lawyer and the client fail to agree on a fee there is an adversarial procedure, which is decided on by the judge to whom the case is referred.

Unless some other agreement has been reached or the client has been ordered to pay costs, fees are based on the tentative fees set by the Bar Association for the province in question, applied in accordance with the Association's rules, practice and customs.

Clients who do not have the necessary means to pay for lawyers' and court lawyers' services can request free legal aid.

How to become a lawyer in Switzerland

Damiano CANAPA[116]

Introduction

From an outsider's perspective it could seem natural that in a small country like Switzerland, a qualified lawyer from one Canton can represent clients in all Swiss judicial authorities.

However for more than 150 years, the federal structure of the State constituted a barrier to this vision. In fact, during all these years, there was no regulation providing the freedom of movement to lawyers in the country. This situation lasted for two main reasons. First the Cantons had a strong attachment to their lawyer's education, and secondly, throughout the twentieth century each Canton kept distinct laws of procedure (the unified Swiss Civil Procedure Code and Criminal Procedure Code only entered into force on 1 January 2011).

A lawyer, who wished to represent clients before jurisdictions in a Canton other than that in which he had qualified, therefore needed specific Cantonal Authorisation from the second Canton. Practically, this created a cumbersome system whereby a lawyer who wanted to practice nationally needed to make individual requests in all the twenty-six Cantons.[117]

---

116 LL.M. (Bruges), Research Assistant (University of Zurich), Lawyer. The author kindly thanks Benoît Chappuis, former Chairman of the Geneva Bar Association, for his critical review, as well as Adam Czewoja Sheikh for his linguistic review.

117 Swiss Federal Council, Message concernant la loi fédérale sur la libre circulation des avocats, 28 April 1999, BBL/FF 1999, pp. 5331 ff., 5335 (hereafter: Message).

Over the years, the evolution of Swiss Federal jurisprudence, as well as the adoption of the Federal Act on the Internal Market[118] facilitated a lawyer's the ability to receive Cantonal Authorisations.

Paradoxically, through the entry into force of the Bilateral Agreement on the Free Movement of Persons,[119] which was notably meant to simplify and harmonise judicial qualifications, Swiss-trained lawyers were continuously subject to Cantonal Authorisation, while foreign-trained European lawyers were exempted. Swiss lawyers therefore suffered a reverse discrimination in comparison to their colleagues from the European Union (EU) or European Free Trade Association (EFTA) who may not have had knowledge of Swiss law.[120]

The Federal Act on the Freedom of Movement of Lawyers of 23 June 2000 (FAFML),[121] which entered into force on 1 June 2002, introduced a paradigm shift in the way Swiss qualified lawyers could practice. For the first time, a federal law introduced minimum standards governing the "qualification as a lawyer in Switzerland"[122] and gave Swiss-qualified lawyers the right to practice freely throughout the country. Furthermore, the Swiss legislators transposed the principles issued by the European Directives 77/249[123] (for the possibility to

118 Classified Compilation of Federal Legislation (SR/RS) 943.02. This Act is still in force today and continues to play an important role for the free movement of lawyers.

119 Agreement between the Swiss Confederation, of the one part, and the European Community and its Member States, of the other, on the free movement of persons, SR/RS 0.142.112.681.

120 On the aspect of reverse discrimination see François Bohnet/Vincent Martenet, Droit de la profession d'avocat, Bern 2009, para. 591 ff. (hereafter: Bohnet/Martenet).

121 SR/RS 935.61.

122 The education that one receives after university in order to qualify as a lawyer admitted to the bar.

123 Council Directive 77/249/EEC of 22 March 1977 to facilitate the effective exercise by lawyers of freedom to provide services, OJ L 78, 26.3.1977, p. 17.

provide services), 89/48[124] (for the aptitude test), and 98/5[125] (for the permanent legal practice under the professional title of the home Member State),[126] into the FAFML. Together, these initiatives established the free movement of European Lawyers in Switzerland.

After a general introduction on the FAFML, this paper will focus on the conditions needed to qualify as a lawyer in Switzerland, as well as on the conditions that enable the free movement of European Lawyers and Non-European Lawyers in the country.

The Federal Act on the freedom of movement of lawyers

The FAFML regulates the free movement of lawyers in Switzerland and outlines the principles that govern legal practice in the country (Article 1 FAFML). Every lawyer that is registered in a Cantonal Register of Lawyers has the ability to represent clients in legal proceedings before all Swiss judicial authorities within the lawyer's monopoly (Article 4 FAFML).[127] The result is that contrary to the situation prior to the entry into force of the FAFML, it is now no longer necessary for a Swiss lawyer to require a Cantonal Authorisation from a Canton in which he is not registered if he wishes to represent a client before its judicial authorities. The only proof that a Canton may still require

---

124 Council Directive 89/48/EEC of 21 December 1988 on a general system for the recognition of higher-education diplomas awarded on completion of professional education and training of at least three years' duration, OJ L 19, 24.1.1989, p. 16.

125 Directive 98/5/EC of the European Parliament and of the Council of 16 February 1998 to facilitate practice of the profession of lawyer on a permanent basis in a Member State other than that in which the qualification was obtained, OJ L 77, 14.3.1998, p. 36.

126 Message, p. 5375.

127 The extent of the lawyer's monopoly to represent clients in legal proceedings is ruled by Article 68 Swiss Civil Procedure Code (SR/RS 272), Article 127 Swiss Criminal Procedure Code (SR/RS 312), Article 40 Federal Supreme Court Act (SR/RS 173.110) as well as, alternatively (cf. Article 3 para. 2 FAFML), by cantonal law (cantonal monopolies, *e.g.* in the field of administrative law).

from a Swiss lawyer is his inscription in a Cantonal Register of Lawyers anywhere in Switzerland.[128]

The FAFML applies to lawyers who pursue activities relating to the representation of a client in legal proceedings before judicial authorities in Switzerland. It outlines the prescriptions under which lawyers, who are either an EU or EFTA Member State national, may represent clients before Swiss judicial authorities. These prescriptions also apply to Swiss nationals who qualified as lawyers in a Member State of the EU or of the EFTA (Article 2 FAFML – the FAFML contains in annex a list of professional titles identifying who qualifies as a lawyer in each EU and EFTA Member State). It is therefore important to underline that the FAFML only governs the free movement of Swiss and European lawyers for their activities relating to the representation or defence of clients before judicial authorities. In contrast, there are no legal restrictions on the activity of offering legal advice, which means that anybody, even people without a legal training, can offer services in this field.[129]

The FAFML does not regulate exhaustively the qualification as a lawyer in Switzerland. Article 3 FAFML states that the Cantons have sole jurisdiction over this process. The FAFML does, however, set the minimal standards in relation to the mandatory professional and personal requirements in order for a lawyer who is qualified in a Canton to benefit from freedom of movement in the whole country. At the same time, these minimal standards constitute the maximal standards that a Canton can request in order to allow lawyers that have qualified in other Cantons to represent clients before its judicial authorities.

In addition, the FAFML calls for the creation and maintenance of a Cantonal Register of Lawyers by each Canton. In order to benefit from freedom of movement, lawyers qualified in Switzerland who intend to pursue activities relating to the representation of a client in

---

128 Yvan Jeanneret, Commentaire de l'article 4 LLCA, in: Michel Valticos/Christian Reiser/Benoît Chappuis, Commentaire Romand, Loi sur les avocats, Bâle 2010, N. 5 f. (hereafter: Jeanneret).

129 François Bohnet, Droit des professions judiciaires, 2nd ed., Neuchâtel 2011, p. 36 f. (hereafter: Bohnet).

legal proceedings before judicial authorities and who fulfil the minimal professional and personal requirements set by the law (see below *Qualification as a lawyer in Switzerland*), must register with the Register of the Canton in which they have their main business address (Articles 5 and 6 FAFML). At any point in time, if a lawyer no longer meets one of the professional or personal requirements, he will be deleted from the Register and will not be admissible to represent clients in legal proceedings before judicial authorities.[130] The Cantons may also create other categories of Registers that regulate the representation in judicial proceedings before their own authorities, *e.g.* a Register for Trainee Lawyers. People that are registered in this second category of Register will, however, not benefit from the freedom of movement foreseen by Article 4 FAFML, but only from a potential free movement governed by cantonal law.[131]

Finally, the FAFML has unified the rules of professional conduct and disciplinary supervision applicable in Switzerland in an exhaustive manner. These rules are outlined in Articles 12 and 13 FAFML. They include the obligation for the lawyer to practice independently, with care and diligence, and to avoid conflicts of interest. The lawyer is also subject to the professional secrecy, which is not limited in time, in all matters entrusted by its clients in the practice of his profession. As soon as a lawyer is registered in a Cantonal Register of Lawyers and is accordingly entitled to move freely in the entire country, he is subject to the rules of professional conduct be it for representation in legal proceeding or legal advice.[132] These rules must be followed both by Swiss and by EU or EFTA Member State qualified lawyers active in the country (see below *Qualification as a lawyer in Switzerland*).

130 Bohnet/Martenet, para. 704 ff.
131 BGE/ATF (Judgement of the Swiss Federal Supreme Court) 125 II 315; Jeanneret, N. 2; Bohnet, p. 33.
132 Bohnet/Martenet, para. 1112 ff.

Qualification as a lawyer in Switzerland

Generally speaking, the FAFML sets minimal professional and personal requirements for the lawyer's qualification in Switzerland and regulates the use of the professional title of lawyer.

Professional requirements

In order to grant a lawyer's licence enabling the registration in any Cantonal Register of Lawyers, and subsequently the right to free movement in Switzerland, two professional requirements must be met (Article 7 FAFML).

First, it is necessary to hold a law degree awarded by a Swiss university (licence or master), or an equivalent diploma awarded by a university of a country that has concluded an agreement of mutual recognition of diplomas with Switzerland.[133] It is necessary to have both the equivalence of the diploma and the agreement of mutual recognition of diplomas. Therefore, it would not be compatible with the wording of the FAFML to limit access to the qualification as a lawyer to holders of a diploma in Swiss law. In addition to the criterion of a law degree awarded by the University of a country that has concluded an agreement of mutual recognition with Switzerland, a Canton may however also require that a lawyer passes a complementary exam of skills in Swiss law and the proof of acquisition of some possible missing knowledge before it gives access to its lawyer's qualification.[134] For the accession to the lawyer's training, only the equivalent diplomas awarded by universities of EU or EFTA Member States have currently to be recognised by the Cantons under the FAFML. In

133 An exception to this rule is made for the Cantons in which Italian is the official language (Ticino and Graubünden); they may independently recognize an equivalent foreign diploma that was achieved in Italian. The Canton of Ticino made use of provision.

134 Bohnet, p. 24

fact, Switzerland only concluded agreements of mutual recognition of diplomas with these countries.[135]

Second, the lawyer's qualification must consist of at least one year of practical experience (lawyer's internship), followed by an exam testing theoretical and practical legal knowledge (bar exam). Whilst a bachelor in law is sufficient to start the internship, a master in law is required to pass the bar exam. The length of the lawyer's internship varies between Cantons. Generally, two years is the norm in French speaking Switzerland, and only one year in the German speaking Cantons.[136] However in the latter, preparation for the bar exam requires often more time.[137] All together, the process of qualification as a lawyer in Switzerland usually lasts around two years everywhere in the country.

In order to enable the free movement of lawyers in Switzerland, the FAFML only sets minimal standards with regard to the lawyer's qualification (see above *The Federal Act on the freedom of movement of lawyers*). The Cantons, therefore, remain free to fix their requirements in order to qualify as a lawyer on their territory (Article 3 FAFML) and, in particular, may foresee stricter conditions. Because a cantonal legislation may not limit the free movement of lawyers that fulfil the requirements set by the FAFML, lawyers who qualify under

135 Ernst Staehelin/Christian Oetiker, Kommentar Artikel 7 BGFA, in: Walter Fellmann, Gaudenz Zindel, Kommentar zum Anwaltsgesetz, 2nd ed., Zurich/Basel/Geneva 2011, N. 9.

136 In bilingual Cantons, the length of the internship is usually influenced by the dominant language.

137 Bohnet/Martenet, para. 530 ff., 535 ff., 537 ff. For instance, in the Canton of Zurich the internship lasts 12 months and can take place in any part of the cantonal judicial system (law firm, Court, Attorney General); 18 months in the Canton of Bern of which 9 must be undertaken in a law firm and 3 in a Tribunal or with a Public procurator; 24 months in the Canton of Geneva with one semester of "Lawyers' School" and a minimum of 12 months in a law firm from the Canton; and 24 months in the Canton of Vaud of which a maximum of 6 months may be accomplished in another Canton or in a judicial authority (Court, Public procurator). See Philippe Meier/Christian Reiser, Commentaire de l'article 7 LLCA, in: Michel Valticos/Christian Reiser/Benoît Chappuis, Commentaire Romand, Loi sur les avocats, Bâle 2010, N. 44.

such stricter cantonal rules will of course also benefit from the freedom of movement in the whole country.[138]

Conversely Cantons may establish an alleged bar exam, or an access to their lawyer's qualification to holders of diplomas awarded by universities from States that have not concluded an agreement of mutual recognition of diplomas with Switzerland. A lawyer qualifying under such cantonal rules will admittedly have the right to represent clients before the judicial authorities of the Canton of qualification. However, he will not benefit from the freedom of movement provided by the FAFML. In fact, the conditions of Article 7 FAFML will not be fulfilled in such a case. For this reason, he will not have the right to register in a Cantonal Register of Lawyers.[139]

Personal requirements

The personal requirements that have to be met by lawyers in order to register in the Cantonal Register of Lawyers are listed in Article 8 FAFML. According to this article, lawyers must practice independently. This requirement, which is the most fundamental, means that lawyers may only be employed by individuals that are themselves registered in a Cantonal Register of Lawyers.[140] In fact, the obligation to practice independently is both a personal requirement that has to be fulfilled in order to register in the Cantonal Register of Lawyers and a professional rule according to Article 12 FAFML. Furthermore, lawyers must have the civil capacity to act, and they must not have been convicted of acts that are deemed incompatible with the profession of lawyer. In the case where a lawyer has been subject to a criminal conviction, this must be deleted from their judicial record. Finally, the lawyer cannot have an act of insolvency against them.

---

138 This situation may create some Canton registration shopping, as some people will prefer to qualify as a lawyer in a Canton which has lower standards.

139 Message [note 1], p. 5367; Bohnet, pp. 20, 25.

140 Lawyers who are employed by a recognised charity organisation may however register with a Cantonal Register of Lawyers provided that they limit their activity of representation to the mandate of their organisation (Article 8 para. 2 FAFML).

Professional title

A lawyer must use the professional title he was awarded in the Canton in which he passed his bar exam or the equivalent professional title of the Canton in which he is registered. In his business relations, he must, in addition, indicate the registration to his Cantonal Register of Lawyers (Article 11 FAFML). This last rule was introduced in order to differentiate between lawyers active within the lawyer's monopoly and representing clients before judicial authorities, and lawyers having passed the bar exam but working, for instance, as legal advisers in an undertaking.[141] The FAFML does not protect the wording of the professional title awarded by the Cantons. However, a person that would use such a title without being entitled to it would be subject to sanctions based on cantonal legislation as well as on the Swiss Criminal Code[142] or the Swiss Unfair Competition Act[143].[144]

Free movement of European lawyers in Switzerland

Lawyers who are EU or EFTA Member State nationals and who are qualified lawyers in their home Member State[145] under one of the professional titles listed in the Annex of the FAFML,[146] *i.e. European Lawyers*, are placed into three distinct categories. First, the ability to provide services in Switzerland; second, their permanent legal practice

141 Bohnet/Martenet, para. 729 ss.

142 SR/RS 311.

143 SR/RS 241.

144 Jean Heim/Pierre-Dominique Schupp/Béatrice Hurni, Commentaire de l'article 11 LLCA, in: Michel Valticos/Christian Reiser/Benoît Chappuis, Commentaire Romand, Loi sur les avocats, Bâle 2010, N. 3 ff.

145 *I.e.*, the State of the EU or EFTA in which they achieved their lawyers' qualification.

146 *E.g.*: *Rechtsanwalt* in Austria and Germany, *Avocat* in France, *Avvocato* in Italy, *Advocat* in Norway, *Adwokat* or *Radca prawny* in Poland, *Abogado*, *Advocat*, *Avogado* or *Abokatu* in Spain, and *Advocate*, *Barrister* or *Sollicitor* in the United Kingdom. This list is identical to the lists incorporated in the European Directives 77/249 and 98/5.

in the country under their original professional title; and third, their inscription in a Cantonal Register of Lawyers. As a reminder, these rules also apply to Swiss nationals who are qualified lawyers in a Member State of the EU or of the EFTA (see above *The Federal Act on the freedom of movement of lawyers*).

Possibility to provide services

A European Lawyer may pursue activities relating to the representation of a client in legal proceedings before all judicial authorities in Switzerland in the form of services (Article 21 FAFML). In fact, the federal and cantonal judicial authorities before which the European Lawyer intends to act, as well as the Cantonal Supervisory Authorities, may not request from a European Lawyer providing services in Switzerland proof that he holds a Swiss authorization to practice. They have the right, however, to ask him to demonstrate his qualification as a lawyer in his home Member State (Article 22 FAFML). The freedom to provide services is however limited to 90 days of effective work per calendar year, according to Article 5 and Annex I of the Bilateral Agreement on the Free Movement of Persons.

A European Lawyer providing services is not registered in the Cantonal Register of Lawyers. He must adopt the professional title of his home Member State, expressed in one of the official languages of that State, with an indication of the name of the professional organization through which he is authorized to practice, or by the name of the court of law before which he is entitled to practice, pursuant to the laws of that State (Article 24 FAFML).

He shall, however, work in conjunction with a lawyer who is registered to a Cantonal Register of Lawyers for the pursuit of activities relating to the mandatory assistance by a lawyer (Article 23 FAFML).[147] However, following the judgement of the Court of Justice of the European Union in the case *Commission v Germany,*[148] the obligation to work in conjunction with a domestic lawyer does not mean

147 The assistance of a lawyer is mandatory in cases of severe breach of the law.
148 Case C-427/85, [1988] 1123.

that the domestic lawyer has to represent the client. It is simply a formality, which obliges the European Lawyer to have an address in the law firm of a registered lawyer.[149]

A European Lawyer who provides services in Switzerland is generally subject to the rules of professional conduct provided by Articles 12 and 13 FAFML (Article 25 FAFML).[150] In the case of a breach of these rules, the Cantonal Supervisory Authority may take disciplinary measures against the European Lawyer and shall notify the competent authority of his home Member State of any measure taken (Article 26 FAFML).

Permanent legal practice in Switzerland

After having registered with the Cantonal Register of European Lawyers of the Canton in which he has a professional address, a European Lawyer may pursue, on a permanent basis and under the professional title of his home Member State, activities relating to the representation of clients in legal proceedings before all the judicial authorities of Switzerland (Article 27 FAFML). In order to register, the European Lawyer shall present to the Cantonal Supervisory Authority a certificate which is not older than three months and which attests his registration with the competent authority of his home Member State. In the case that a European Lawyer has more than one business address, he shall register in the Canton in which his main business is located.[151] The Supervisory Authority must then inform the competent authority of the home Member State about the registration (Article 28 FAFML).

Before initiating a disciplinary proceeding against a European Layer who is registered in a Cantonal Register of European Lawyers, the Cantonal Supervisory Authority shall inform the competent au-

---

149 Message, p. 5377.

150 See above*The Federal Act on the freedom of movement of lawyers* .

151 Benoît Chappuis/Olivier Mach, Commentaire de l'article 28 LLCA, in: Michel Valticos/Christian Reiser/Benoît Chappuis, Commentaire Romand, Loi sur les avocats, Bâle 2010, N. 3; Andreas Kellerhals/Tobias Baumgartner, Kommentar Artikel 28 BGFA, in: Walter Fellmann, Gaudenz Zindel, Kommentar zum Anwaltsgesetz, 2nd ed., Zurich 2011, N. 2.

thority in the home Member State and cooperate with it throughout the disciplinary proceeding (Article 29 FAFML).

Furthermore, the rules applicable in the case of the freedom to provide services (Articles 23-25 FAFML, see above Free movement of European lawyers in Switzerland, Possibility to provide services) remain applicable.

Inscription in a Cantonal Register of Lawyers

A European Lawyer may register with a Cantonal Register of Lawyers without fulfilling the requirements described in Part II. if (1) he has passed an aptitude test, or (2) he has been registered for a period of at least three years with a Cantonal Register of European Lawyers, according to the requirements described above (see *Free movement of European lawyers in Switzerland, Permanent legal practice in Switzerland*). In the second instance, (i) the European Lawyer must justify an effective and regular activity in Swiss law during the three-year period, *or* (ii) if within the three-year period he pursued an effective and regular activity in Swiss law of a period less than three years, he must successfully pass an interview in order to assess his professional competences (Article 30 FAFML).

If a European Lawyer is registered in a Cantonal Register of Lawyers, in addition to the professional title of his home Member State he may use the professional title of the Canton in which he is registered (Article 33 FAFML). As such he has exactly the same rights and obligations as a registered lawyer holding a cantonal lawyer's qualification.

Three-year registration with a Cantonal Register of European Lawyers

If a European Lawyer has been registered with a Cantonal Register of European Lawyers for three years, and that he can justify an effective and regular activity in Swiss law during that period, he can request registration to a Cantonal Register of Lawyers without any further examination.

If, on the contrary, the lawyer can only justify practice in Swiss law for a shorter period of time during that three-year period, he may pass an interview in order to assess his professional competences. The rules for this are set out in Article 32 FAFML. Following the wording of this article, the Lawyers' Examining Commission of the Canton in which the European Lawyer wishes to register is the competent authority to conduct the evaluation. The evaluation is notably based on the information and documents that relate to the European Lawyer's professional activity in Switzerland. By providing these documents, the European Lawyer must demonstrate his effective and regular activity in Swiss law.[152] Any knowledge and professional experience, as well as continued professional education in Swiss law, such as attendance at lectures and seminars, is also taken into account.

Aptitude test

Article 31 FAFML sets out the criteria for an aptitude test. In order to be eligible to sit this this test, European Lawyers must have successfully completed studies lasting at least three years in a university. They must also hold a diploma required for the designation of lawyer in an EU or EFTA Member State. The aptitude test, which can be passed at anytime, can be retaken up to two times. It is also organised by the Lawyers' Examining Commission of the Canton in which the European Lawyer wishes to register. The exam itself shall consist of matters that are covered by the cantonal bar exam, and that differ substantially from those covered by the education received by the European Lawyer in his home State. The test shall also take into account the professional experience of the candidate.

Free movement of non-European lawyers

Lawyers who do not have the nationality of an EU or EFTA Member State and who did not qualify in Switzerland are excluded from the

152 Bohnet/Martenet, para. 863 ff.

personal scope of application of the FAFML (see above). This exclusion is also extended to Swiss nationals who did not qualify in Switzerland or in an EU or EFTA Member State. Because of this, such lawyers cannot register in a Cantonal Register of Lawyers or in a Cantonal Register of European Lawyers, and subsequently, cannot pursue activities relating to the representation of clients in legal proceedings before the judicial authorities of Switzerland on a permanent basis.[153]

As an exception to this principle, Cantons may however foresee, on the basis of Article 3 FAFML, that non-European lawyers may represent clients in legal proceedings before their cantonal judicial authorities. This can be done through an individual cantonal system of authorization.[154] It is however unclear whether the rules of professional conduct, disciplinary supervision, and sanctions provided by the FAFML would apply.[155]

However, lawyers who do not have the nationality of an EU or EFTA Member State, but who are qualified in an EU or EFTA Member State under one of the professional titles listed in the Annex of the FAFML, shall have the possibility to provide services in Switzerland if they are employed by a Swiss law firm.[156]

Conclusion

With the entry into force of the FAFML, minimal requirements for the lawyers' qualification and practice in Switzerland were established for

153 For a general analysis of the relationship existing between FAFML and GATS cf. Message, p. 5384 ff.; Bohnet/Martenet, para. 117 ff.

154 Dominique Dreyer, Introduction aux articles 21 à 26, in: Michel Valticos/Christian Reiser/Benoît Chappuis, Commentaire Romand, Loi sur les avocats, Bâle 2010, N.14 ff., 19.

155 Bohnet/Martenet, para. 229.

156 Hans Nater/Michael Tuchschmid, Die internationale Freizügigkeit nach dem Bundesgesetz über die Freizügigkeit der Anwältinnen und Anwälte, in: Daniel Thürer/Rolf H. Weber/Wolfgang Portmann/Andreas Kellerhals, Bilaterale Verträge I & II, Schweiz – EU, Handbuch, N. 27, footnote 44; Bohnet/Martenet, para. 814.

the first time on a federal level. This law has a dual aspect, as it regulates national as well as international situations.

On a national level, the conditions of the Swiss lawyers' qualification were unified for the first time. Such a development was essential in order to enable lawyers who had qualified in Switzerland to move freely in the whole country. At the same time Cantons maintain the ability to determine the lawyers' education that shall apply in their territory. In fact, with regard to the conditions of registration in a Cantonal Register of Lawyers and the free movement of lawyers, only minimal conditions are foreseen by the law. This is done in accordance with the federal system that governs the country.

On an international level, in the general context of the right of European Lawyers to practice freely within Europe, the FAFML prevents Switzerland from becoming an isolated island in the middle of an increasingly unified continent. In fact, the law integrates the conditions issued by the Bilateral Agreement on the Free Movement of Persons under which European Lawyers can practice in Switzerland on a permanent or non-permanent basis.

The process for becoming an attorney in the United States

Charles F. SZYMANSKI[157]

Introduction

While the legal profession in the United States has come under increasing criticism over the past 20 years in public opinion surveys, becoming an attorney has still remained a desirable – and highly competitive – career choice for many students. Thus, while parents may on one hand criticize lawyers at a dinner party, at the same time they often encourage their children to become a lawyer.

Becoming a licensed attorney in the United States is a three-step process: 1) meeting the requirements for entering law school, 2) successfully completing law school, and 3) obtaining a license to practice law. Each step will be explained in more detail below.

Requirements to enter law school

For the vast majority of individuals seeking to become a lawyer, admission into an American Bar Association (ABA) accredited law school is the first prerequisite. While non-accredited law schools do exist (particularly in California), graduates of such schools are often not eligible to sit for many states' bar examinations, and consequently have limited prospects to obtain a license to practice law upon graduation.

---

157 Professor, Vytatuas Magnus University, Faculty of Law, and licensed attorney, State of Michigan, United States.

In order to eligible to attend an ABA accredited school, the applicant must have successfully completed at least a bachelor's degree (in the U.S., a four year course of study) in any subject, and have taken the Law School Admission Test (LSAT). It is also usual for law schools to require that applicants submit letters of recommendation and a short essay describing why they wish to study law. The requirement of a bachelor's degree is a minimum requirement; individuals with master's degrees or even doctorates are also free to apply. Interestingly, it is rare for a law school applicant to have an undergraduate degree in law or legal studies. Those holding bachelor's degrees in political science are common among applicants, but even degrees in music, theater, or chemistry are not entirely unusual.

The LSAT is a national test administered by the Law School Admissions Council (LSAC), and is currently held three times per year, in June, October and December. Typically, the test is held on a Saturday, but there alternate calendar dates for those who are unable to take the test on Saturday due to religious reasons. Law school admissions decisions are typically made in December-March timeframe, and so applicants should take the exam sufficiently in advance to ensure that their scores will be made available to the law schools prior to this period. The LSAT is scored on a 120 to 180 point scale, with 180 being the highest possible mark, and 120 the lowest. The test is graded on a curve, so most significant for applicants is the percentile in which their score falls. Thus, a score in the 90th percentile means that this individual has performed better than 90% of all other people taking the same exam.

While the law school admissions process is not entirely based on a mathematical grid, the use of such a table is the basis for most admissions decisions. The admissions grid has two variables: the students' grade point average (GPA) and LSAT score. In the United States, GPAs range from 0 to 4.0 (4 being the highest mark in American universities, with 3 being considered "good" and 2 "fair"). Thus, a student with a 4.0 GPA has achieved perfect marks in all of his or her classes. An applicant with a 4.0 GPA and an LSAT score in the 99th percentile is assured admission into the vast majority of U.S. law schools, and has an excellent chance of getting into the very best law schools (such as Harvard or Yale). A 3.0 GPA combined with an LSAT score in the 75th percentile can likely achieve admission into the middle-tier of U.S. law schools. Applicants with GPAs in the 2.0 – 2.5 range, with an LSAT score below the 50th percentile may have difficulties in being admitted.

Again, though, there are factors that can create exceptional circumstances and would justify a departure from relying entirely on such an admissions grid. This may include the quality of the applicant's school (i.e., a bachelor's degree from Harvard is given a higher value than an unknown or poorly regarded university, so that a 3.0 GPA from Harvard is seen as superior than a 4.0 at the unknown college), some kind of special life experience (growing up in poverty, being an accomplished musician, providing famine relief for an NGO in Africa, etc.), and perhaps extraordinary letters of recommendation.

In earlier times, a person's race and gender could also be considered as a factor in admission decisions (and so members of minority groups might receive a "plus" in admissions consideration), but constitutional legal developments have changed this practice.

While most applicants are either simply accepted or rejected by law schools, some are put on a waiting list for admission. When a law school sends out acceptance letters, it is not sure precisely how many applicants will actually decide to enroll at the school. If less applicants enroll than expected, vacancies are created and these are filled by applicants on the waiting list.

It should be emphasized that the entire application process, from the applicants' perspective, is strongly driven by the desire to get into the best law school possible. Which law school is in fact best is measured by general academic reputation, and increasingly magazine rankings (taking into account not only reputation but also selectivity, placement, resources, etc.). Often, the better the law school, the better the graduates' prospects are for finding a high-paying legal job. Of course, numerous applicants choose law schools for family and/or geographic reasons (they live in Atlanta, with their spouse and family, and therefore would like to go to a school in Atlanta), and for financial reasons (they cannot afford an excellent but hugely expensive private law school), but perhaps there is a greater willingness among applicants to relocate or take out additional loans to attend a more highly regarded law school.

Completing law school

Law School in the U.S. is a professional program leading to a doctorate in law (most often called a Juris Doctor, or J.D.). It is comprised of a three or four year program, requiring the completion of approximately 90 credit hours of study. A typical credit hour is one hour of weekly classroom instruction over the course of the semester. Thus, a three credit course would meet for three hours each week over a 15 week semester, amounting to a total of 45 classroom hours. The ABA sets minimum requirements for accreditation purposes, but there is some flexibility offered in each law school's curriculum.

The first year of studies in law school consists mostly of required courses. These typically include: Civil Procedure, Torts, Property, Criminal Law and Procedure, Legal Writing and Contracts. Some of these subjects are semester length courses, while others are offered as year-long subjects. Constitutional Law is also often required, but sometimes may be taken in the second, rather than first, year of studies. Recent trends have seen the inclusion of International Law as a required subject in the first year curriculum, reflecting the growing importance of that subject, even in the United States.

In the second year, there still may be some requirements to fulfill (often Professional Responsibility, Corporations, Federal Income Taxation, among other courses), but students may begin to choose electives that are more interesting to them, or relate to their future plans of specialization. The third year usually consists entirely of elective courses, although students may satisfy the requirement to take a writing seminar that last year. Such seminars require the student to complete a substantial research paper.

Skills and clinical courses are becoming more and more common in second and third year law school curriculums. In skills courses, such as Trial Practice or Advocacy, or Moot Court, students learn how to try a case before a jury, and how to practice in appellate courts.

Legal clinics offer students the opportunity to actually represent clients under the supervision of a law professor, in typically low value cases (low monetary value, but still of high importance to low income or elderly clients). Sometimes students receive credit for internships (working at a public agency or non-profit during the summer) or externships (performing such legal work during the academic year). The idea is to provide law students with some practical skills so that they will have an idea how to practice law upon graduation and upon receiving their law license, without the need for a formal apprenticeship.

In order to graduate, students must attain at least a 2.0 GPA and pass enough courses to satisfy the school's credit hour requirement, including all required courses. Still, this is the bare minimum. Grades are critical for students' efforts to find jobs. The higher a student's GPA, in general, the greater ease for him or her to find a quality legal position upon graduation. This reality creates a highly competitive environment among students during law school. On the other hand, it also may contribute to greater student attentiveness and effort during class, increasing the quality of their studies.

While most law schools operate a three year program, some offer a four year "night" program for students who are working or otherwise unable to attend law school full-time.

Obtaining a license to practice law

Obtaining a Juris Doctor degree from an ABA accredited law school does not entitle one to practice law.[158] It simply makes the individual eligible to sit for a state bar examination.[159] Graduation from law school typically takes place in May, and the bar examinations are held

158 With one exception: the state of Wisconsin allows law graduates from its two law schools to waive into the bar without an examination, so long as certain course and other requirements are met.

159 In addition, foreign lawyers who graduate from a U.S. post-graduate LLM program (a one year program, often in U.S. law) may sit for the New York bar exam.

at the end of July. There is no one license to practice law throughout the United States. Graduates must select the particular state or states in which they wish to practice and work, and apply to sit for that state's (or those states') bar examination(s).

In addition to the requirement of obtaining a law degree from an ABA accredited law school, applicants to the bar exam must also submit to certain ethics or moral character requirements. Most states require a criminal background check for those wishing to take the exam. In addition, 46 states require applicants to have achieved a passing score on the Multistate Professional Responsibility Examination (MPRE), which tests their knowledge of legal ethics. There is no one, uniform passing score for the MPRE; instead, each state sets the score which it deems to be passing. Sometimes it is enough to have taken the MPRE before registering for the bar exam, even if the results are issued after the bar exam itself.

The bar exam itself varies in content and form from state to state. Most often, however, the examination consists of two parts and his held over the course of two days. One part is the Multistate Bar Exam (MBE). This is a multiple choice, national examination, which covers the core subjects (i.e., Contracts, Constitutional Law, Torts, Property, Criminal Law, and Evidence) required in law school. It consists of 200 questions. Those completing the MBE receive a raw score (based on the number of correct answers) and a scaled score (which is higher, and takes into account the difficulty of a particular exam). Each state may determine what minimum MBE scaled score is necessary to pass. Typically, a score of 135 or more is considered good.

The second part of the exam is held on a different day and consists of essay questions, and typically focuses on the specific state's law in various subjects (including additional subjects not on the MBE).

In order to pass the entire exam, the state may require a minimum combined score on the essay and MBE portions, a minimum score in for each part, or a very high MBE score (in which case the individual automatically passes and the essay part of the exam is not graded).

As a practical matter, a person may sit for a maximum of two states' bar exams during the summer. Thus, one could take the Pennsylvania essay exam on one day, the MBE the next day, and the New Jersey essay exam the third consecutive day. The MBE results would count towards both states' respective examinations. Some states allow a person who successfully passes one state's bar examination to waive in (or be admitted without examination) to their respective bar. Sometimes such states impose additional requirements as well, including attaining a specific minimum score on the MBE, or a substantial number of years of practice as a licensed attorney in the other state. Other states do not have any waiver provision, however, and to be admitted into the bar of those states, one must sit for and pass a bar examination.

The results of the July bar examination are given the following November or even December. Successful individuals are then sworn in as licensed attorneys in a special ceremony shortly thereafter. Some states have more difficult exams than others; traditionally, New York and California have had lower bar passage rates, with only 50% of exam takers passing the exam.

Once an attorney receives his or her license, he or she is fully qualified to practice law in that state. There is no apprenticeship requirement for U.S. attorneys. Moreover, there is no distinct qualification requirements for different categories of legal professions. Thus, a licensed attorney may theoretically become a prosecutor, a trial lawyer (trying cases before judges and juries), a transactional lawyer (drafting and negotiating contracts and documents, a law professor or even a judge without additional education, experience or examinations.

Of course, a law professor, in fact, will often have exceptional academic qualifications and a publishing record before being hired at a law school. Judges in the Unite States are either elected by the people in a popular vote or are appointed (by a governor of a state, or for federal judges, by the President). Often these are, in fact, very experienced lawyers, and upon becoming a judge have the opportunity for additional, specialized judicial training.

For attorneys who would like to practice law with the federal government (for example, at a federal agency in Washington, D.C.), they must be admitted to the bar of any state. There is no special federal bar examination.

Conclusion

Some of the unique features of the process of becoming a lawyer in the United States include high competitiveness (competition to be admitted into the best law school, and among students to achieve the best grades while in school); the unified, professional structure of legal education (there is no master's degree, only a doctorate, and graduation plus bar passage entitles one to practice any legal profession, from professor to judge to trial advocate); and the lack of any apprenticeship requirement (which is somewhat offset by the heavy use of clinical and legal skills courses in law school).

The system appears to be working and generally produces qualified and competent attorneys, who operate in an advanced, complex legal system. The most recent crisis in the process of becoming a lawyer in the U.S. is not really due to structural, systemic problems in legal education, but simply is based on financial reasons. Law school is not only very competitive, but is extremely expensive. Students may finish law school with more than $150,000 in debt. While compensation for lawyers has traditionally been much higher than other fields, this staggering potential debt load – combined with a stagnation in the employment market for lawyers – may ultimately lead many aspirants to the legal profession to reconsider their career choice.

So you want to be a lawyer in California (USA)

Frank ROMANO

Introduction

A dichotomy exists during the path taken by the prospective California lawyer. On the one hand, the California Bar exam, a passing score necessary to practice law in California is one of the most difficult to pass in the US. On the other hand, California offers more options for becoming a California lawyer than most states.

I. Preliminary requirements

Pre-law school education

Most US states require a BA or BS degree in any subject which is normally a 4 year program and is equivalent to a license in France. However, a few states, such as California, allow a candidate to take the bar who has a minimum of two years of college credits or has worked at least four years under the personal supervision of a judge or a California attorney in his law firm, the latter having practiced law in California for at least five years.

The requirement of a BA degree in any subject in the US is strikingly different than what French students are faced with. They must decide whether or not to study law the first year of university. Thus there is no grace period. As such, while French students are registering for school after high school they must declare whether they wish to enter law school and take courses in that specialty as early as the first day of class.

In fact, in the US system, the university student, not only does not have to declare whether he desires to enter law school before the first day of university classes, but only has to choose a "major", or specialty area, after the second year of university studies (i.e. English, history, etc.). In addition if the student envisages attending law school he does not have to start preparation, i.e. sending in applications until the last year of the four year undergraduate (BA or BS) program. As such, American students are far less pressured to choose a specialty at an early age than French students.

Also, American students are accepted to study law school at a comparatively later age, even after having worked for several years. The reason behind that is assumed that older students are more motivated to overcome the challenges of law school than recent high school graduates. Perhaps the latter are more inclined to drop out after the first year than older, more mature students.

Law school admissions test

Notwithstanding exceptions noted above and below, a student may apply to law school in the States in the last year of university and only upon obtaining a BA or BS degree and passing the LSAT, the Law School Admission Test. During the last year, the candidate will usually take a preparatory course which lasts at least 2-3 months before the exam. Since most students take an LSAT preparatory class, in order to have the greatest possibility to obtain a competitive score, they are almost required to take the preparatory course. Their options for choosing law schools are directly proportional to their scores on the LSAT.

The exam lasts about four and a half hours and tests analytical reasoning, reading comprehension and writing skills. With respect to analytical reasoning skills, the test measures one's ability to determine relationships between concepts, comprehend the impact of rules on decisions, analyze a set of facts and conclude after following guidelines. It determines the ability to ferret out main points of arguments, apply logic to abstract concepts, find relevant information within a text, and analyze and evaluate arguments.

The reading comprehension section tests the ability to read a text and make inferences as well as identify main ideas and locate relevant information in intricate, scholarly texts.

Finally, the essay section requires the candidate to write a short essay developing an argumentation based on a text.

Once the student passes the LSAT, it's time to consider law schools. The biggest decision is whether to go to an ABA (American Bar Association) approved or a non-ABA approved law school.

II. Law school options

ABA approved law schools

First of all, it is a decided advantage for the candidate to attend an ABA law school. However, there are also advantages to a non-ABA approved law school that will be discussed below. The ABA is a national organization and provides for accreditation of law schools and services for lawyers, namely sponsoring courses for continuing legal education and other services. There are about 200 ABA accredited law schools. They are the most prestigious law schools in the US. As such, entrance into them is more difficult than non-ABA schools.

Apart from the added prestige there is a specific advantage to obtaining a law degree from an ABA law school. That allows the degree holder to apply to take the bar exam in any state in the United States. Provided that the bar exam is passed of that state, the person can practice law there.

State approved law schools and programs

Some states provide opportunities to become a lawyer other than by attending an ABA school and passing the bar exam. Candidates can also qualify to take the local bar exam and thus to practice law after attending a non-ABA school which is a state accredited law school. In some states, notably in California, candidates can even qualify to take the bar exam by working for a judge or an attorney without attending any law school. Those latter options will be discussed below.

As stated above, some States have their own accredited law schools which are not approved by the ABA law schools. They can be organized like a typical ABA law school, with classrooms, conference rooms, and libraries or can organize the courses in a correspondence school framework. Some require only 2 years of university before allowing admittance into their program while others require a BA or BS degree after 4 years of study at a post high school institution.

However, graduates of a non-ABA law school, with few exceptions, are only authorized to take the bar exam of the state in which the law school is located. Thus the candidate can only practice in that state as opposed to students from ABA schools who can practice law in any state in which he successfully passes the bar exam.

In addition, after one year of studying in those schools, they are required to pass the so-called Baby Bar. It is the first stage in the process of a student in a non-ABA approved school. That means he must pass the exam in order to pass on to the second year of law studies in that school. If not, he must repeat the first year and take the Baby Bar again before continuing to the second year.

According to the California Bar Examiners "The ABA schools have significantly higher pass rates on the California bar exam than do the California CBE schools – all of which is transparent on the State Bar website. They also have different student bodies and other differences that provide opportunities as well as requiring careful regulation. Some of the California Bar Examiner's (CBE) schools are less expensive and some, individually, are more expensive than the ABA schools."[160]

In addition, the CBE claims that the non-ABA accredited law schools are claiming some advantages over ABA schools. For example, "they claim to have expanded the technological developments in teaching law giving them rights to claim they have."[161] Some claim that non-ABA schools have the "most sophisticated distance learning

160 "A fresh look at California's law schools," by Howard B. Miller, President, State Bar of California, California Bar Journal, August 2010, <http://www.calbarjournal.com/August2010/Opinion/FromthePresident.aspx>.

161 Ibid.

system in the U.S. [and] may also have the most credentialed student body of any law school in the country. At its graduation two years ago, the valedictorian of the class was a graduate of the Indian Institute of Technology (the equivalent of Caltech or MIT) with a Ph.D. in electrical engineering from U.C. Berkeley. He was not unique. In the graduating class were more Ph.D.'s, MD's and MBA's than I have seen at any other law school".[162]

That indicates that due to the distance learning programs, more candidates who are already engaged in a profession and cannot attend a full-time day program of the ABA (there are very few ABA night programs) and are made up predominantly of mid-career adults.[163] These schools are faced with a modern dilemma: in this age of increasing need for electronic legal research[164] over books, should they maintain their expensive libraries. Even though it still is useful for a lawyer to understand how to use a library and a card catalogue, it is not nearly as essential as learning how to perform research electronically.

Given the growing use and necessity of understanding technology by lawyers, according to one author, one of the things the California Bar must address is "how functional is its continued insistence of fixed facilities libraries with standard and expensive volumes of books. Certainly in today's world the ability of a lawyer to search electronically is far more important than knowing how to use a card catalog or thumb through a physical book volume. Both are useful; one today is essential…"[165]

In spite of the differences stated above between ABA and non-ABA schools, the classroom education in both frameworks is organized similarly.

---

162 Ibid.

163 Ibid.

164 Electronic legal research is defined as research using data bases such as Lexis and Westlaw.

165 Supra, P. 1.

The classroom framework of ABA and non-ABA schools

Both ABA and non-ABA school practice what is called the "Socratic method," which revolves around a dialogue between the professor and the student. For example, the professor will engage a discussion concerning an important U. S. Supreme Court case and then question students about the details, often following up with further questions on the facts as well as on the reasoning of the judges. It becomes a dialogue as opposed to a classical lecture by a professor on the law.

This contrasts with the French method, at least in the lecture courses, where French law students mainly take notes in a large amphitheater with very little, and often no discussion between the professor and students.

However, most lecture courses in a French law school are linked to smaller discussion groups (called TD, or travaux dirigés) with about 30-35 students. In those settings, the students engage in a discourse with the professor as well as sometimes give oral reports on legal issues. The method however, even in the small groups often does not follow the Socratic method of the American law schools since there is rarely a Socratic dialogue, i.e. questions and answers and the professor's follow-up with further questions to the student with which he is engaged in dialogue.

Another difference between French and American law schools is that American law students, from the very first day, learn to draft legal documents such as legal memoranda, and briefs to be submitted to the courts. This greatly distinguishes the quality of education in American law schools from French law schools and confirms that the former are far more practically oriented. In contrast, the French law student normally will never learn how to draft legal documents in the four years of attendance before obtaining the first French law degree (Maîtrise de droit) which is equivalent to the American law degree (JD- Juris Doctorate).

However the French student, after obtaining his Maîtrise de droit, in order to practice law, must pass a very competitive Bar Exam (C.R.F.P.A.-usually about 20% of the candidates pass the test). After passing that exam, he enters EFB (Ecole de formation au barreau), the

French Bar school where he will finally learn the practical aspects of the legal profession, i.e. how to draft legal memoranda, briefs, etc.

Law school education: Correspondence school

Some states in including California allow candidates to study law by correspondence school. California allows this with conditions, in particular, the school must require at least 864 hours of study over a four-year period.[166]

After the candidate has satisfied those requirements, he will be allowed to take the state bar examination.

Non-law school candidates

It still remains that in most states, the only way to become a lawyer is to obtain a diploma from an ABA accredited law school and pass the bar exam.

However, in California, candidates may qualify to take the Bar exam by working in a law firm or for a judge in Judge's chambers without going to an accredited law school. The principle is that the candidates have sufficient education working on practical projects, legal research and/or writing briefs or legal memorandums to qualify as a lawyer without attending a law school.[167] In order to qualify to practice law after working in a law office or judge's chambers, the following requirements must be satisfied:

- completion of the requisite pre-legal and legal education;
- registration as a law student;
- passage or exemption from the First-Year Law Students' Examination;
- a positive moral character determination;
- passage of the Multistate Professional Responsibility Examination; and

166 <http://www.calbar.ca.gov/LinkClick.aspx?fileticket=sTLIEzERQUM%3D&tabid=2662>.

167 <http://admissions.calbar.ca.gov/Education/LegalEducation/LawOfficeorJudgesChamber.aspx>.

– passage of the California Bar Examination. Additionally, an applicant must not be certified by the State Department of Social Services as being in non-compliance with a court ordered child or family support obligation[168].

To begin the procedure in California, the candidate must file, under Rule 4.16[169], as a law student. However, in that case, the legal education will be provided by a law firm or Judge's chambers experience.

That does not mean, however, automatic acceptance as a lawyer after completing that program. Applicants must file an initial report not later than 30 days following the commencement of law office/judge's chambers study. Following that initial report, candidates must file a report approximately every 6 months. The candidate, under personal supervision of a lawyer or judge, must show in a report signed by the candidate or judge he worked with, the cases studied and other legal matters and procedures studied and legal work performed, i.e. drafting briefs, complaints, legal memoranda, etc. In other words, the candidates must prove that they have performed tasks similar to ones performed by lawyers.

A similar procedure exists in France whereby a jurist[170] who works for several years in a law firm may qualify to become a member of a French Bar.[171]

III. The Bar examination

The exam and duration

For all states in the united states, the final step before becoming a lawyer is to take and pass a bar exam that lasts at least two days (in

168 Ibid.

169 Rules of the State Bar of California, Title 4 - Admissions and Educational Standards.

170 A person who graduated with a Maîtrise de droit or completed a Master's program in France.

171 <http://afje.org/content/la-passerelle>.

California, three days), six or seven hours per day. In California, it is even more of a test of attrition and even fortitude in order to be able to keep up the momentum during the three long days of testing. The bar exam typically consists of three sections:

- Hypothetical cases to resolve,
- a multiple choice test (MBE) and
- the Performance test.

The hypothetical cases sections is a page or so of facts that the candidate must read and resolve the main legal issues by an accurate reading of the facts and knowledge of the law. The MBE part of the exam tests the candidates knowledge of the law and the performance part of the exam requires the candidate to, in a very short period of time, read a stack of documents (in a typical law firm file) and then draft a complaint or an appellate brief.

To prepare for the California Bar exam, candidates typically register for an expensive preparation course that lasts two months.

In addition, to become a lawyer in any state, the student must pass the state bar exam. There is no federal bar exam. Thus for a California lawyer to be able to systematically practice in another state, such as New York, he must pass the New York Bar. However if he has a case in a different state, he has to request permission to argue the case, exceptionally. Usually the request is granted.

Finally, once the bar exam is passed, the candidate will take the oath during a ceremony and will be considered a full-fledged lawyer, and can even create his own law firm.

Foreign candidates

With a first degree of law

For those foreign candidates who have obtained a first degree in law, to be eligible to take the California bar exam, they must submit an application for equivalency to the Bar Examiners. To be eligible to take the exam, they will be required to show that their education was equivalent to the one provided by an American law school and have completed one year of studies in an ABA approved law school.[172]

Without first degree of law

For those law students who studied law outside the US without obtaining a qualifying first degree in law, to be eligible to take the California Bar, they must complete successfully at least two years of undergraduate studies, pass or show exemption from the 1sth year law students exam (Baby Bar, discussed above) and complete 4 years of legal studies in the US.

Conclusion

In light off the above, in spite of the challenges to becoming a California attorney and of the fact that the California Bar is arguably the most difficult due to the lowest bar-pass rates in the union, California ironically provides more opportunities to become a lawyer than most states.

---

172 <http://admissions.calbar.ca.gov/Education/LegalEducation/ForeignEducation.aspx>.

LIST OF AUTHORS

Ajani, Gianmaria

Professor, Dean of the Department of Law, University of Torino, Italy
Lawyer

Bastida, Daniel

Professor, Rector of the University of Andorra

Brandl, Ulrike

Dr., Associate Professor, University of Salzburg, Department of Public Law/Public International Law

Canapa, Damiano

LL.M. (Bruges), Research Assistant (University of Zurich), Lawyer

Dursi, Anthony

United Kingdom - Recruitment & Outreach Manager
The Honourable Society of the Inner Temple

Franco, Raquel

Lawyer at LCA Advogados, Lisbon

Gunputh, Rajendra Parsad

Associate Professor (Law), Faculty of Law and Management
Head-Law, University of Mauritius

Kopa, JU Dr. Martin

Doctoral Researcher
Palacky University in Olomouc, Faculty of Law, Department of Constitutional

Kraśnicka, Dr. Izabela

Faculty of Law, University of Bialystok

d'Oliveira Martins & Guilherme Waldemar

Lawyer, Part time lecturer Faculdade de Direito da Universida de Lisboa

Rascagneres, Joan Miquel

Lawyer, President of the Andorra Bar Association

Rohlfing-Dijoux, Stéphanie

Professor, Director of the bilingual Master 2 European Law – German Law
University Paris Ouest-Nanterre-La Défense
Member of the Paris and Munich Bar

Romano, Frank

Assistant Tenured Professor (Maître des conférences)
University Paris Ouest-Nanterre-La Défense
Adjunct Professor- Golden Gate University Law School, San Francisco
Member of the California and Marseille Bars

Schlüter, Claudia Dr. iur.

Technische Universität Dresden; Law Faculty; Institute for Intellectual Property, Competition and Media Law (IGEWeM); Head of the Erasmus Office

Seul, Otmar

Professor emeritus of the University Paris Ouest-Nanterre-La Défense,
Coordinator of the Network of European Universities in legal studies

Skomerska-Muchowska, Izabela

Assistent Professor, University of Lodz

Szymanski, Charles F.

Professor, Vytatuas Magnus University, Faculty of Law and licensed attorney,
State of Michigan, United States.

Tomoszek, Ph.D. JU Dr. Maxim

Senior Lecturer
Palacky University in Olomouc, Faculty of Law, Department of Constitutional Law, director of Centre for Clinical Legal Education

Trocan, Laura Magdalena

Ph.D. University Lecturer – Faculty of International Relations, Law and Administrative Sciences, University „ Constantin Brâncuşi„ of Târgu-Jiu, Romania, Researcher Associate at the Legal Research Institute „ Acad. Andrei Rădulescu" of Romanian Academy of Bucharest

Cultures juridiques et politiques

Vol. 1 Stephanie Rohlfing-Dijoux (éd)
La Transmission de Terminologie et de Concepts Juridiques dans l'espace Européen. *Allemagne / France / Russie*
2012, ISBN 978-3-0343-1094-9

Vol. 2 Otmar Seul & Tomas Davulis (éds./Hrsg.)
La Solidarité dans l'union Européenne / Solidarität in der Europäischen Union. *Actes de la 5ème Université d'été franco-germano-lituanienne et européenne en sciences juridiques Vilnius, 3-10 juillet 2008 / Tagungsband der 5. Deutsch-Französisch-Litauischen und Europäischen Sommeruniversität in den Rechtswissenschaften, Vilnius 3.-10. Juli 2008*
2012, ISBN 978-3-0343-1122-9

Vol. 3 Ralf Alleweldt, Raphaël Callsen, Jeanne Dupendant (eds.)
Human rights abuses in the contemporary world.
Tri-National Workshop, Tbilisi, September 2011
2012, ISBN 978-3-0343-1147-2

Vol. 4 Stefanie Bouquet
La réglementation européenne relative à la discrimination fondée sur l'âge: conséquences sur le droit du travail français.
Préface du Professeur Joachim Gruber, Université Paris Ouest - Nanterre La Défense
2012, ISBN 978-3-0343-1174-8

Vol. 5 Izabela Kraśnicka & Magdalena Perkowska (éds.)
How to become a layer?
2013, ISBN 978-3-0343-1290-5

www.ingramcontent.com/pod-product-compliance
Ingram Content Group UK Ltd.
Pitfield, Milton Keynes, MK11 3LW, UK
UKHW021849100926
8556IPUK00020B/1138

9 783034 312905